palmistry

Anna Comerford

palmistry

The art of reading palms

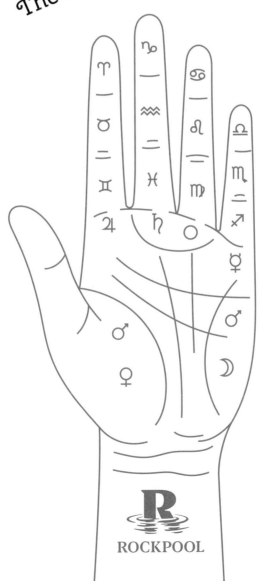

ROCKPOOL

To all the divine hands who will open themselves to you like a budding lotus
ready to awaken to their full potential . . .

A Rockpool book

PO Box 252
Summer Hill
NSW 2130
Australia

rockpoolpublishing.co

Follow us! f ⊚ rockpoolpublishing
Tag your images with #rockpoolpublishing

ISBN: 9781925946215

Published in 2021 by Rockpool Publishing
Copyright text © Anna Comerford 2021
Copyright design © Rockpool Publishing 2021

Adobe stock images, pages 80, 82, 101, 120, 126, 128, 139, 143, 153, 162, 164
Illustrations by Carissa Harris, pages 10, 15, 20, 41, 58, 66, 86, 94, 99, 107
Author image by Carly Taylor

Design and typesetting by Dana Brown, Rockpool Publishing
Edited by Lisa Macken

NATIONAL
LIBRARY
OF AUSTRALIA

A catalogue record for this
book is available from the
National Library of Australia

Printed and bound in China
10 9 8 7 6 5 4 3 2 1

'Thank you, Anna, so much for your amazing information and insights on palmistry! Although I am already a practising psychic medium I have become more accurate and successful in my palmistry readings with clients, and the feedback I receive from them is excellent!' — Diane

'I am so glad I took your course as it has helped me to become a more precise psychic reader. I love my work more as I can now see how palmistry helps people and guides them in their lives.' — Sarah

'Thanks, Anna, for an amazing palmistry course. I enjoyed every moment of it and learnt a lot from you and the other wonderful and awesome students.' — Peter

'I am loving palmistry more and more and feel that it resonates with me. I now do my card readings together with palmistry. I feel that you can really tell a lot about a person by reading their palm, even more in depth than the cards.' — Claire

'Thank you, Anna, for reading my palm. It brought tears to my eyes as you really tapped into me and my life. I am telling my friends about you!' — Jenny

'Your palmistry readings are accurate and heartfelt. Thank you, Anna, for your sincerity.' — Grace

Contents

Introduction

Thank you for choosing this book, which will change your life just as palmistry has changed mine. It's not only a book about the magic of palms, it's also a book about energy, focus and the wisdom in your hands. I tell my students that every line or mark has a positive message in it, just like every experience in life has a gift and message for us. How you perceive little bumps along the way will determine how you roll along your life's path: you can choose to be a victim or you can choose to be a creator. The lines and marks on your palms can change just as your thoughts and beliefs do. Every cell and every line on the palm is part of your essence, part of who you are.

Palmistry, or chiromancy as it is also known, is from the Greek word *kheir* meaning 'hand' and *manteia* meaning 'divination', which means foretelling the future through the study of the palm. Palm reading is also known as chirology. Those who practise chiromancy are generally called palmists, palm readers, hand readers, hand analysts or orchirologists.

Palmistry is the practice of reading the lines and markings on the palm of the hand. The study of palms began in ancient India and spread to other parts of the world: the Egyptians and Greeks began practising palmistry over 5,000 years ago, then in the 17th century the foundations into the techniques of palmistry were more fully laid. Palm reading was revived in the 19th century when mystics began using its divination practices. In the 20th century psychiatrist and psychoanalyst Carl Jung was impressed by palmistry as he felt it was an amazing skill that used facts along with intuition and insight; he had his palms read several times.

The book covers a comprehensive list of topics that will provide you with the knowledge and skills to proficiently and expertly perform palmistry readings, topics such as timing, scrying, hand reflexology and meridians and the unusual lines you will come across in your search to unravel the mysteries of the palm. I have also included chakras and psychic senses in the book, along with information on performing a palmistry reading that has helped me read palms at fairs, at my home practice and in the courses I teach. To be a fabulous palm reader you need to be in tune psychically and energetically; therefore, I have included exercises in this book to help you tap into guides, higher

intuition and the energy of the palm. At the end of the book are some examples of palm readings for you as well as a checklist to help you identify the markings on the palm.

Many former students who are now professionally reading palms have given me great feedback about how this information has helped them to master palmistry. I wish I had been able to find a book like this many moons ago, *before* my years of reading palms and teaching palmistry. I have read many books on palmistry over the years – and I still find it an enthralling subject – and 30 years ago when I was in my mid 20s I delightfully read the palms of family members and friends. My understanding of palmistry, spirituality and energy has developed considerably, so it is pure joy for me to share these insights with you.

My students are often amazed at how different palmistry books believe different things about palmistry. I suggest you experiment and see what feels right for you and what style of palmistry works for you, as in the end you will be the person who is performing the reading. Your own intuition and perceptions will guide you to identify what the fingers and palms represent for you and your client. Calling on your client's spirit guide, as well as your own, to help interpret the palm is a powerful way to get an accurate reading.

Reading the palm is a journey that goes beyond the conscious mind. When you trek into your subconscious world, where symbols and messages dwell, you will find your readings become alive and you will become a more powerful reader. If you are reading this book I predict that you are a naturally inquisitive, intuitive and curious person; it's likely that you look beneath the surface of situations, that you like to see beyond what's presented to you and enjoy digging deeper into it.

We were all born with exquisite hands, and you owe it to yourself to understand the lines and shapes of your hands. My wish is for you to use the knowledge in this book to learn about the magnificent art and magic of palmistry; may you shine brightly as you awaken and expand your natural intuitive and psychic gifts.

When you read palms from your heart, the experience of palmistry is energising, fulfilling and fun. Welcome to this exciting journey!

Chapter 1

The hands

Palm reading, or palmistry, is an ancient art of fortune telling that the Chinese are believed to have begun using 5,000 years ago. The science of palmistry was also studied by the Romans, Greeks, Indians and Egyptians.

Palm reading consists of observing the lines of the palm and other features on the hands. Chiromancy means reading the palms and interpreting the lines on the palm. Looking at a person's palm can unveil a detailed picture of their life and how they relate to the world around them. Palmistry can reveal how a person will interact with others in love, work and play.

⮞ Hand facts ⮜

Did you know that hands begin to form about four weeks after conception? By the end of the fourth month the lines, ridges and creases on the fingers and palms will be fully formed to reveal a person's own unique identity. Palmistry

is a way of interpreting these lines to assist in identifying a person's behavioural patterns, health and lifestyle.

Did you know that the lines on a palm are called flexion creases? These creases, or lines, can reveal our path in life and the path we have ahead of us. Also, the lines can make us aware of the changes we can make in order to create a more harmonious and fulfilling life.

Dominant and non-dominant hand

Are you right-handed or left-handed? The hand you write with is your **dominant** hand, while the other is your **non-dominant** hand. If you write and perform major tasks with your right hand it is your dominant hand and the left is your non-dominant hand, and vice versa if you write/perform tasks with your left hand. One of my clients said she was ambidextrous, but after discussing it she acknowledged that her right hand was the one she wrote with the most so her right hand became the dominant hand in the reading.

The non-dominant hand represents the traits and gifts you are born with and indicates family patterns and genetics, while the non-dominant hand represents your

growth and development and how you expand your traits and gifts.

When I read a person's non-dominant hand I sometimes get a flash of a past-life aspect; these aspects may be reflected in the client's current life. Your soul may heal past-life memories and experiences by giving you the opportunity to make wiser decisions in this lifetime so you can create better outcomes. While reading one client's hand I saw an image of her fighting in a war scene where there was conflict and struggles. She acknowledged that this made sense as she felt she was 'at war' with so many people and circumstances in her current life. I believe I was shown this image so I could speak with her about how she was manifesting these situations in her life and what she needed to do to change them. When we do things differently, powerful changes can occur.

My years of experience indicate that the non-dominant hand represents approximately the first 40 years of a person's life, while the dominant hand represents from about age 40 onwards. This belief is not set in stone, so tune in to your own intuition and see what feels right for you and the person you are reading. My palmistry students often ask me if they should only read one hand (the non-dominant hand) if the person is under 40 years of age, but it's important to read both hands as each hand will tell a story and give you guidance about the person's life.

Passive non-dominant hand	Active dominant hand
• The past • Family and hereditary influence • What you came into this world with • Your potential, gifts and abilities	• The present and the future • How you use your talents, gifts and abilities in this lifetime • What you are learning in this lifetime

Hand shapes

Fire hand   **Earth hand**   **Air hand**   **Water hand**

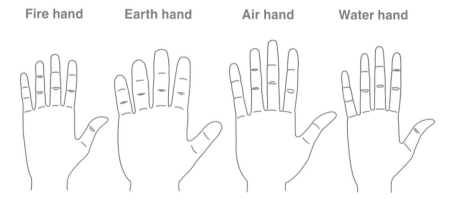

The shape of the hand reveals a person's character. There are four elements associated with the shape of hands, with most hands being a combination of those four:

- *Earth*: the palms are broad and square in shape. The length of the palms may be similar in length to the fingers, or the fingers are stocky and short. People with square/earth hands are earthy, honest, industrious and realistic.
- *Air*: the palms are a square-type shape, and the fingers may be longer than the palms or slender. People with air hands are compassionate, affectionate and very intuitive.
- *Fire*: the palms are a rectangular shape. The fingers may be shorter than the palms and knotted, with bony finger joints. People with fire hands are intellectual and like to learn, and also creative and full of new ideas.
- *Water*: the palms are a rectangular shape and may be long and flexible. The fingers may be the same length or longer than the palm. People with water hands are sensitive, social and artistic.

Empty hands

An empty hand is a palm with only a few visible lines. I've found they appear on younger people, then over time the lines deepen and become more pronounced. Empty-handed people are reliable but they may procrastinate, not completing tasks on time and being slow to make up their minds.

Observe if the empty lines are on both hands or if one hand has deeper or more lines than the other. Remember that the non-dominant hand represents what gifts people are born with and the dominant hand is how they use their gifts in a productive and purposeful way. If the lines on a person's non-dominant hand appear faint yet the lines on their dominant hand are deeper and stronger, then the person will most likely improve and excel in this lifetime.

⌐ The empty hand ⌐

Recently when I was giving readings at a psychic fair one of my palmistry students, Lyn, was in attendance integrating her knowledge of palmistry into her psychic readings. During our lunch break Lyn informed me that one of her clients had hardly any lines on her palms. Some clients may have naturally pale hands or only a few faint lines on their hands; some palmists feel an empty hand means the person needs more grounding. However, I feel it could be hereditary or indicate that the person energetically needs more joy in their life so the lines will create more colour and vitality in them!

I did a palmistry reading for a 22-year-old girl, Larissa, who presented with faint lines and whitish hands. Larissa admitted she was having health problems, that she always felt tired and fatigued and that she had been suffering from an eating disorder, and she agreed to have a blood test. My advice was for Larissa to get her iron tested along with a general blood test to see how everything was functioning for her.

Note: always recommend to clients that they check with their doctor or health-care professional before they make any changes to medications or their health plan. It's also important to remember that advising the use of herbs seems reasonable enough but some herbal remedies interact in adverse ways to particular medications. Clients need to see their doctor or health-care professional before they ingest any type of herbal medicines.

Palm colour

Palms should normally be a rosy pink in colour. Cold, clammy hands could indicate the person's overall health needs to be looked at. If the palm is pale it could be a sign of anaemia (low iron levels) so suggest the client see a doctor for a blood test, especially if they haven't had one recently.

Timing

Timing, which refers to at what age events occur in a person's life, is a very interesting part of palmistry. Palmists read time in different ways depending on their belief systems and experience. When I was learning palmistry various books said various things, especially about the heart line. Some books said the heart line should be read from the Mercury (little) finger side of the palm while other books suggested it should be read from the other end. After some trial and error I decided to read the start of the heart line as beginning from the side percussion edge, under the Mercury finger.

As with other contentious issues, always tune in intuitively to the timing on people's hands as you'll be surprised at how accurate you can be. If a client does not connect with an age you've shared with them move on to another area of the palm, as you are only human and your timing may be slightly out or the client may not recall certain life events.

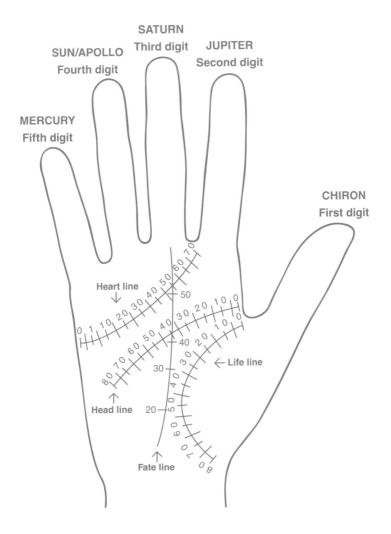

Timing tips: it is useful to imagine a line going down from the middle of the Jupiter (index) finger till it meets the life line, as it will represent from 16 to 18 years of age. A line going down from in between Jupiter and Saturn (middle finger) will meet the life line at approximately 22 to 24 years of age. The fate line meets the head line at approximately 35 to 40 years of age, and the fate line meets the heart line at approximately 50 to 55 years of age.

⟿ Red dots ⟾

Ralph, a tall, 40-year-old male who was keen to get a palmistry reading, sat down in my clinic one lovely sunny day. He had long palms and brittle nails, and when I peered through the magnifying glass I noticed a red dot on his life line. I tuned in to the energy of this dot to sense the timeline, and I felt the dot represented a distressing event around the age of 34. Ralph admitted he had tried to take his own life at age 35 but luckily his girlfriend had found him in time. He had since received counselling and was getting his life back on track.

Exercise 1: *timing*

Study the timing diagram on page 15 to get acquainted with the way timing is calculated on the palm.

Observe the lines on your own palm to get a feel for the timings on the hand. Ask family members and friends if they would like to volunteer their palm so you can practise the way timing shows up on the palm. Look for any markings and other areas of interest that stand out for you. Sometimes, reading someone you already know helps you to confirm the dates and times of significant events that have happened in that person's life.

Practise asking your guide or superconscious to help you ascertain timing on the palm. Also ask for help in determining what certain lines or markings mean. Remember, some people may forget when certain events occurred or it may dawn on them later. Tap in to your intuition and the natural psychic ability we all have to give you pertinent information. Good luck!

Chapter 2

Major lines of the palm

By looking at the major lines of the palm you can assess how well you or your client is keeping everything in balance. The major lines in palmistry are the life line, the heart line and the head line, which represent the mind, body and soul respectively. The heart line is where your soul speaks to you; your soul connects with you through your heart chakra. The head line is associated with your mind and your thoughts, while the life line represents vitality and energy.

Life line

The life line, which is also known as the vitality line, represents resilience, physical health, vitality and general well-being. It is one of the most controversial lines in palmistry, and a common mistake some palm readers

19

make is suggesting a short life line indicates a short life. This is not necessarily true.

The life line starts from the edge of the palm, above the thumb, and runs towards the wrist, usually forming a beautiful arc. It highlights the relationship you have with your family and depicts your energy levels. A broken or split life line could suggest the person will encounter a shift or change in their life around the time the life line splits on the palm. If the life line is broken it may mean the person will experience a change in lifestyle and that their soul will guide them onto a different path.

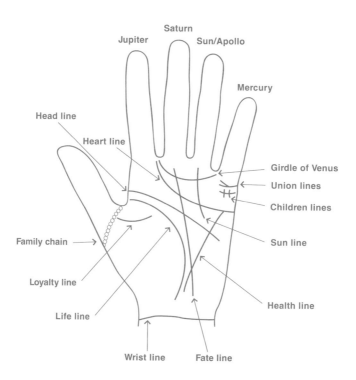

Some people have an additional inner line that is shorter than the main life line, which indicates there's extra energy being given to that person. This inner line is known as the Mars or sister line, and can represent added support from a family member or friend or from someone who has crossed over who wants to help and guide the person you are reading. You may like to tune into the energy of this spirit via mediumship so you can connect with the loved one who has crossed over and pass on any messages they may have for your client. I find that some spirits are keen to chat and pass on messages and may do so through any of the seven clairs (see Chapter 10).

Most people have a curved life line; the more curved it is the more passionate the person is about life. The closer in to the thumb area the life line is the more cautious the person is about life. If you see that the head line is more visible and deeper than the life line it may indicate the person is more mentally than physically active. A person who loves travel and variety may have a life line that sways out to the centre bottom of the palm towards the wrist area. I did a palmistry reading for Steve, aged 69, whose life line reached out into the Neptune mount (see Chapter 7) in the middle of the wrist area. Steve confirmed that he loved to travel and had completed many trips around the globe.

Heart line

The heart line represents your heart and emotions, revealing how you interact, respond and relate to emotions and the people around you. It is found on the palm just below the fingers, running from below the little finger towards the index finger. The heart line runs horizontally across the upper palm, passing the mounts of Mercury, Apollo and Saturn (see Chapter 7).

If the heart line is straight the person is more emotionally controlled and has a matter-of-fact personality. If it is curved the person is emotive and sensual. A broken heart line may mean the person has experienced a challenging emotional time, especially around the timeframe the break appears on the heart line.

Most people I see have lines that end between the Saturn (middle) and Jupiter (index) fingers, which indicates a person who falls in love easily. One of your lessons on earth is discerning who to engage with emotionally; challenging relationships are your greatest teachers as they may push you into a different direction and life path. Relationships can help to clear up past karma so your soul can then move on to other suitable relationships or friendships.

If the heart line is clear and deep the person is sincere, respectful and considerate. An absent heart line may reveal

a person who is more logical and based in reason and can also reveal traumas and pain from previous generations. Find out if there is any grief or deep emotional blocks that are being held on to, as family patterns could be blocking the heart line from being present. I have seen clients heal past family pain and burdens by doing energetic healing (the conscious and skilled use of therapeutic modalities such as reiki, reflexology and kinesiology). Even if a client does not know what happened to their ancestors, you can still send love, light and healing to the past to help release it from your client's DNA and energy field. Past-life burdens can be released in the same way, as negative patterns usually provide a chance to heal the past and create healthier behaviours and thought forms.

The length of the heart line may reflect a person's attitude to relationships. A short line could show a person who is self-focused, so this lifetime will be about learning to understand other people's points of view. They may also need to learn to allow space in their life for love, connection and companionship. A long heart line indicates a person with an idealistic view of love, so much so that they have high expectations of it. They may need to learn to be realistic by understanding that many people are imperfect and have flaws, and that the art of negotiation and communication will assist people in their relationships.

You will find conflicting ideas by palmists about the timeline of the heart line. Some palmists believe the heart line timeline should begin from the edge of the palm, while others think it should start from the other end. I gauge the timeline of the heart line as starting from the outer edge of the palm, as I find this is a better way to assess timeframes.

Curved heart line

In palmistry, people who have a curved heart line are more romantic; they like displaying their feelings and emotions to others through cards, gifts and flowers. A curvy line also means the person freely expresses their emotions. If the heart line curves towards the head line (which is rare) it may mean the person is intellectually focused in relationships and needs to connect with their heart more.

Straight, short heart line

A person with a straight, short heart line may be more head based than heart based and may need to focus more on developing a connection with their heart.

Straight, long heart line

People with long, linear heart lines are good with other people; they are the carers of the world as they have empathy for the less fortunate. People whose palms have a straight heart line may be more passive in their romance, enjoying the receipt of love but not wearing their heart on their sleeve. They tend to keep their love inside their hearts, so their challenge is to feel safe about opening up to love.

I have sometimes seen a heart line on a non-dominant hand that was quite straight yet the person's future (dominant) hand showed a more curved line, meaning they become more open to their heart's feelings and more comfortable with expressing their emotions as they get older. This is in tune with how we develop as humans: our chakras expand and open as we experience life, especially if we tap into our heart and soul more. See Chapter 11 for more information on the chakras.

Heart line ends under the index finger

If the heart line ends under the Jupiter (index) finger it could indicate a sensitive person who thrives in a healthy and well-suited relationship. They are particular about whom they date and socialise with.

Heart line ends under the middle finger

Although rare to see, a heart line that ends under the middle finger can indicate the person is clingy in love and needs healing around emotional issues to help them relax and trust that they are worthy of love and attention. Are you a giver or taker in love?

I recently read the palm of Adam, a handsome man in his 30s. Adam's heart line pointed towards Saturn and he had a girdle of Venus (see Chapter 4). He said: 'I was always taking in love, but now I want to be a giver of love. I have opened my heart to a whole new level of passion and love in relationships.' It can be scary to be vulnerable and open yourself up to love and intimacy, but it is usually rewarding and results in more awareness and positive outcomes!

⤙ Double lines ⤚

Judy, aged 42, had a big double heart line that was oval shaped and looked almost like a long island. The island covered her heart line from ages six to 12, and she confirmed that those years were challenging as both her parents were alcoholics. Judy's life line also had an extra inner line from around 25 to 35 years of age, which represented help from spirit that was being given to her then. Judy said her nanna had passed when she was 25 and that through mediumship her grandmother was able to come through and share some lovely messages with her.

⤙ Heart fact ⤚

Did you know your heart has more energy than your head? According to HeartMath (bit.ly/2I8EJnM) the heart has 40,000 neurons and is 5,000 times more powerful than the brain. Befriending your heart and acting with kindness and love can bring great success, divinity and peace of mind. If you focus too much on the brain, or the 'monkey mind', it can lead to stress, self-sabotage and sadness. The heart can be your intuitive guide, providing you with deep love and wisdom.

Head line

The head line represents the mind and consciousness. It runs from between the thumb and the index finger and slopes downwards across the palm. The head line indicates a person's artistic abilities and their mental and intellectual sides. If the head line is curved it means the person has more of a creative, artistic mind, whereas if the line is straighter it indicates a more logical, analytical person. A long head line ends past the sun (ring) finger; a short head line lines up with the Saturn (middle) finger.

The head line highlights a person's memory, intelligence and ability to reason. A small fork on the line can mean the person is balanced between imagination and the real world. If there's a wavy line it suggests the person changes their mind a lot. If the head line drops towards the moon/luna area of the palm (see the diagram on page 20) the person is innovative and imaginative. A straight head line means clarity and focus. If the head line is broken it may indicate a more anxious person and can point towards challenges in mental health that in this lifetime the person will have the opportunity to overcome. A short line means the person is practical, but remember that like all the other lines the head line may change over time.

The head line starts in the area above the thumb right near the beginning of the life line, joining the life line in about 80 per cent of people. If they are separate it gives more power to the Jupiter (index) digit, creating more self-confidence and self-reliance, and may indicate the person is independent, impulsive and intuitive. When the head and life lines are joined it could indicate a lack of confidence and a person who is not communicating their needs enough to others. These people need to learn to take the initiative to strive forward in life and create happiness for themselves.

After reading many palms over the years I have come to the conclusion that the 20 per cent of clients that do have separate head and life lines are old souls. They are usually wise and are switched on to their intuition and gut instincts.

If there's a line connecting between the heart and head lines it may mean balance between the head and the heart. Look at the area where the heart line starts to see the approximate age that the head and heart align in the person's lifetime. When you blend the head and heart you will find you have more wisdom, love and compassion for yourself and others, and I feel this will create more abundance and wealth in your life.

I once saw a line connecting the head and heart lines on a man who found it difficult to communicate his feelings, needs and wants, which greatly affected his first marriage. One of his life lessons was to learn to blend the head and heart and make decisions from that space and not just ego alone. Listening more to his heart improved his relationships with his children and new partner.

If there's a dot somewhere along the heart or head line it may mean the person had an intense time at the age the dot appears, so you may want to give an approximate age to the client. For example, I saw a dot on a lady's heart line and said to her: 'I feel something had quite an impact on you around the age of 10.' She looked surprised and said: 'Yes, I found out I had diabetes when I was 10.' Another lady, Sally, had a deep red dot on her head line that I felt occurred around age 17, and Sally confirmed her parents split up then. It was a tumultuous time for everyone but especially for Sally, as she felt trapped between her parents' fury.

Ask your guide for information or help with a timeframe. I often ask my guides to help me out, as they assist by helping me see numbers in my mind's eye or somewhere around me. The guides are there to support you, so just *ask*! They will perhaps give you an image or picture of what went on at a certain time in a client's life. Look at your own hand and practise doing it on yourself, or look at a family member or friend's hand. Even though you know about your family and friends' lives you can still learn more about the palms and how the guides will communicate with you. Experiment and have fun with tuning in to other people's palms – with their consent, of course!

Short head line

People with a short head line are practical and get a lot of things done; they prefer experiencing physical achievements rather than mental ones. A short line may indicate a person with poor memory skills who lacks in concentration, so they need to focus more on these areas to improve them. This person would benefit from meditating to centre their thoughts and increase their mental energy and focus.

I found a short head line on Helen, a lovely elderly lady who was well known to my family. She was straight to the point yet at times found it challenging to see other people's points of view. She had incredible stamina and was more of a go-getter in life.

Long head line

Long head lines are found in people who are clear thinkers and left-brain oriented. They usually mull things over before they take action and focus on what needs to be done. A long and straight line shows a motivated, ambitious person with a flair for business.

Straight head line

Straight head lines are found in people who are straight shooters and have clear, linear thoughts. They like understanding why things happen, are analytical and see things in practical, logical ways.

Curved head line

A curved head line signifies a creative and very artistic person. Several years ago I met Scott at a psychic expo in Sydney. Scott, aged 33, was excited to get a palm reading; he had a huge smile and a bright personality. I was surprised by the shape of the head line on his palm: it was the most curved head line I had ever seen! I psychically tuned in to the line and told him he was artistic and creative to the extent where he dreamt about his designs. He said he was a graphic designer and confirmed that he often dreamt about his creations.

Broken head line

A broken head line could indicate a major event that happened at the time of the break or that the person's thoughts are inconsistent. They may need to learn to channel thoughts and deeds so they align and serve them well in this lifetime.

Chained head line

A chained head line may indicate people who are highly strung emotionally as well as intellectually. These people need to take extra care with mental health and take time out for meditation, relaxation, baths and massages so they can unwind and de-stress.

Forked head line

A forked head line may indicate a person who can see more than one point of view. It can also represent a writer's fork. I told one woman 'You have a writer's fork,' and she said, 'Yes, I have had two books published.' People with a fork at the end of their head line are creative souls who love journalling and writing as a way of expressing themselves.

Floating head line

A floating head line, which is rare to see, is when it's unattached to the side of the palm and means the person is carefree and not overly concerned about what others think. It could also mean the person's early family years were lacking in some aspect.

Head line separate from the life line

A head line completely separated from the life line indicates a person who is adventurous and enthusiastic about life. These people are independent, focused and intuitive.

⤝ Steve and Margaret ⤞

Several years ago a young man, Steve, threw his palm in front of my face and said: 'Tell me when I'm going to die. I won't mind what you tell me, I can handle it.' I took a deep breath and smiled at him. This encounter reminded me of when I delved into the mysteries of palmistry 30 years ago and how I thought the same thing. Then I heard Margaret's story. Margaret was in her late 40s when she went to see a well-known palmist. He looked at her palm and informed her that she would live well into her 80s, yet three months after the reading Margaret's daughter saw the palmist and angrily told him that her mother had died in a car accident two weeks prior.

This story reinforces the fact that we don't have the knowledge to tell someone when they will pass over. Palmistry is not an exact science, and it's unethical to give somebody a time when they will die as it could create unnecessary pain and distress. We have a duty to look out for the emotional well-being of the people who come into our space. It's a privilege to share knowledge, wisdom and insight with another, yet it's vital to do it with love and concern for their well-being. I am sure there are mystics out there who reveal such information, but it's their own karma and integrity they need to answer to.

The universe has a divine plan for all of us. No matter whether your life is destined to be short or long, you should aim to live the best you can each day: to be in your heart, master your emotions, learn from your mistakes and be present in every moment you have on this planet.

'Never predict a time of death.' — Nathaniel Altman

Exercise 2: *four-step activation sequence*

Put on relaxing music if you wish.

- *Rainbow cleanse*: imagine breathing rainbow colours into your body and out into the space around you. This will cleanse your energy field.

- *Beam of light*: imagine a glowing white pillar of light beaming down from the sky above you. Move the light down through your body like a shining beam until it reaches into the earth below you. Imagine the beam of light going into the centre of the earth then returning up through your body and flowing out through the top of your head and up a few metres. Bring the pillar of light down into the earth through your body and up again several times. This powerful light beam will create a vortex of healing, grounding and rejuvenating light that will enlarge and enhance your aura and energy field. Feel the expansion around you.

- *Trance*: close your eyes and take several big, slow belly breaths in and out. Relax your shoulders and body then do this breathing cycle:
  - Breathe in for four seconds
  - Hold your breath for four seconds
  - Now breathe out four seconds
  - Hold your breath for four seconds then repeat the cycle.
- Repeat the breathing cycle five to 10 times so your alpha and theta brain waves are activated. Have the intention that all your chakras are opening up in a healthy way for you. Feel deeply relaxed as you continue to slowly breathe in and out.

  Note: 10 of these deep belly breath cycles will take you into a relaxing alpha/theta trance-like state.
- Ask your spirit guide or higher self to assist you clearly and effectively. Call them in three times, which is very powerful and is like ringing the spirit

hotline to help you. They need three requests so they can connect better with your energy field and vibration.

- Now that you are tuned in, open up your clairs and connect to what you feel, sense, see, know, taste and smell around you.

Note: sometimes I imagine I'm in a rainforest or surrounded by large crystals of energy, which helps me to better tune in to my clairs. Do what feels best for you.

Chapter 3

Minor lines of the palm

The minor lines are important in palmistry as they provide a great deal of information when conducting a reading. The minor lines do not appear on all hands, but the more hands you read the more you will get a feel for them. I have

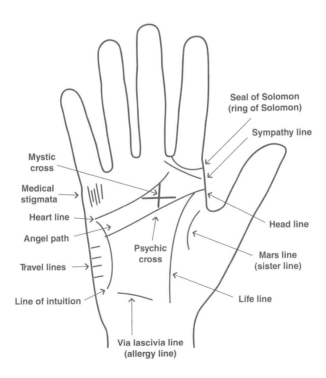

Seal of Solomon (ring of Solomon)

Sympathy line

Mystic cross

Medical stigmata →

Heart line →

Angel path

Travel lines →

Line of intuition

Psychic cross

Head line

Mars line (sister line)

Life line

Via lascivia line (allergy line)

included extra lines and features you may come across that will help you when reading for a client.

Seal of Solomon

The seal of Solomon, also called the ring of Solomon, is a semi-circular line found under the Jupiter (index) finger that can be one curved ring or a double ring. It represents humanitarian achievements, psychic interests and intuitive abilities. The seal of Solomon appears on the hands of psychics, mystics, healers and life and marriage counsellors; in fact, on the hands of around 10 to 15 per cent of the population (Nathaniel Altman, *Palmistry*, Sterling, London, 2009, p. 48).

Loyalty line

The loyalty line is a 1 to 2 cm horizontal or slightly curved line that comes out from the family chain at the base of the thumb. The line reaches towards the life line and sometimes touches it. As the name suggests the line represents loyalty to a tribe, whether it's to family or friends. A person with a loyalty line can be trusted to keep a secret, as they're a terrific confidant.

Sympathy line

The sympathy line is found in the same area as the ring of Solomon – under the Jupiter finger – the difference being that the sympathy line is straight whereas the ring of Solomon is curved. People who have a sympathy line are understanding, compassionate and caring.

Sun line

The sun line, which is also known as the Apollo line, usually appears as a 1 to 2 cm dash or vertical line above the heart line and pointing towards the sun (ring) finger (see the diagram on page 20). It can't always be seen on a hand but when it is it indicates fame, success, abundance, love, beauty, music, art and creating happiness in life. The sun line is also linked with strong creative talent and is found on wealthy and successful people who land on their feet. A long Apollo line is extremely rare and may signify fame.

Some people have two sun lines, which represents great success in two or more endeavours they undertake in their lifetime. In hands where no sun line is present it may mean the person feels they do not deserve happiness, so talk to them about repressed feelings such as not believing they are worthy of success and joy in their life. Ask questions about how their family of origin responds to success and happiness in their lives or whether their family always struggles with the flow of life.

I have seen hands with two close sun lines parallel to each other under the sun finger, and have been surprised to see a third small line crossing over these two lines. I believe this means the person does not believe on a deep level they deserve happiness, success and peace, so if you ever come across this discuss with your client why they think that way. I sometimes do healing around a client's belief system and where it stems from. Hypnosis is useful to get to the core of the issue so they can overcome the block in their lives.

I love it when I see people with crossed-over sun lines on their passive, non-dominant hand but there's no line crossing over the sun line on the active hand. These parallel sun lines represent a pathway that allows flow and abundance into the person's life, so in their future they will clear away the blocks and open up channels to more progress, triumph and joy coming into their lives!

Via lascivia line

The via lascivia line is also called the poison line, the allergy line or the line of Neptune. As you might have guessed, palmistry has several words for many of its lines! The via

lascivia line is short and horizontal and can itself be made up of short lines. It is sometimes difficult to locate: some palmists believe the line exists across the luna mount and points towards Venus, while others say the line is found near the travel lines. Yet other palmists feel it is a short line near the life line that veers towards the luna mount, or you may see it on the luna/moon area of the palm or on the Neptune mount at the base of the palm. I suggest you use your instincts as I have found the line in different areas of the palm.

The via lascivia line indicates the person has issues with lactose, sugar, gluten, food, alcohol or addictions. Some addictions and allergies may be due to blocked emotions, so seeking emotional healing would be advantageous. People with a lot of allergies and food intolerances can be emotionally sensitive. They may have a leaky gut or other health issues that, when healed, help their gut and immune system to be stronger and more resilient. People with allergies to dust, wheat, lactose, cats and so on may exhibit a via lascivia, and they need to be careful about gut health and maintaining a healthy lifestyle.

Some natural healers, naturopaths and homeopaths have the line and are thus drawn to healing themselves and studying in the health arena.

Union lines

Union (or relationship) lines are short horizontal lines found on the edge of the palm between the start of the heart line and the Mercury (little) finger (see the diagram on page 20). You may see one line or several lines. Some palmists believe that if there are two parallel lines very close together it means the client has another close person around such as a work partnership in addition to their main partner.

Union lines indicate close relationships that may be romantic or platonic. They also denote deep friendships and potential relationships, so not all lines may be fulfilled as some people are happy and content in a relationship and do not need to pursue any others.

Children lines

Children lines run vertically across the union lines (see the diagram on page 20). The fact that they represent children makes for controversial theories on where they are located, which is why they are the hardest lines to interpret. It is believed that boy lines are short, straight and vertical while girl lines are slightly curved and shorter and deeper than boy lines. We have more control now over the number of children we choose to have, so you may see more lines in this area than the number of children people actually have. A magnifying glass and a good light may be helpful in determining the delicate children lines.

Someone who has never had children may have children lines as these could represent nieces, nephews or other people's children they have bonded with.

➤ Relationship lines ➤

Jessica returned for a second palmistry reading and asked if we could focus more on her relationship. I tuned in to her aura and her relationship with her boyfriend, Dane, telling her he was keen but that she had one foot in the relationship and one foot out. 'That's spot on!' Jessica tearfully said. She had broken up with Dane several times and was really confused about whether to stay with him or not. He was her first boyfriend, and she felt tremendous guilt each time she broke it off so she would end up going back to him to alleviate her guilt.

The relationship lines on the side of Jessica's palm revealed several relationships, so there were more ahead for her. We looked at the past-life connection she had with Dane and did a visualisation, sending him love, good wishes and healing. After the visualisation Jessica felt less guilt, as it made her realise that releasing Dane in a loving, kind and considerate manner would be fair to both of them. I advised Jessica that it was important to know if guys had the same values as her regarding lifestyle, money, goals and children (she was keen to be a mum). Communicating her needs would help Jessica's soul align with what was best for her and help her connect with someone with similar dreams and goals.

Fate line

The fate line has four names: together with fate, it's also known as the Saturn, destiny and career line. The fate line rises from the base of the palm between the luna/moon and Venus areas and heads towards the mount of Saturn (see the diagram on page 20). If the line points towards the mount of Jupiter it indicates a person who is a natural leader and has a humanitarian mindset. This type of person considers the well-being of others and likes to make a difference in the community. A short fate line does not always mean a short career but may instead mean the person was a late – or early – starter in life.

If the fate line ends towards the sun/Apollo mount it reveals a person on an artistic and creative path in life. A strong, clear fate line indicates that determination, fulfilment and inner confidence will arise in that person's life. If there are breaks in the line it could mean there was or will be a transition or change that occurred around the age where the line breaks. Clients with a break in the fate line may confirm a change of direction in their life such as a new job, moving overseas or having children.

A wavy fate line suggests a path with uncertainty and a lack of direction, but it may also mean the person is willing to ride the wave of life and allow the ebb and flow to decide where they head. If the line has small upward branches coming off it this can mean a successful endeavour, whereas if the line has small branches that go downwards it could indicate a temporary delay or interruption. So-called 'wrong' paths can be fortunate as you will learn many lessons and gain many gifts from these experiences that help you to know more about yourself and your life.

If there are two fate lines side by side it can mean two careers at once or indicate a versatile person who is very capable and has a hobby that is important to them. A faint line could indicate an indecisive and lethargic person who needs to get motivated to bring passion and focus into their life. An absent line may reveal a person with nervous energy, so they may benefit from deep breathing and connecting to the earth to become more grounded and centred in life. Some palm readers believe an absent fate line reveals that the individual is an entrepreneur (or hopes to be) who likes to run their own show.

One of my clients, Samuel, aged 51, had an absent fate line and he admitted he disliked his job. Samuel worked for himself and had always struggled with different jobs over the years; he said he lacked motivation and was working on creating more success and abundance in his life.

A long fate line indicates a person with the energy and determination to complete tasks and reach their goals in life. It shows that a person will have interests and hobbies they enjoy later in life. It's interesting to know that the fate line is connected to Lakshmi, the Indian goddess of wealth, so that a very deep line that is darker than other lines on the palm may reveal an inheritance or business that is passed on.

The fate line crosses the head line at about 35 to 40 years of age and crosses the heart line at approximately 50 to 55 years of age. If the fate line goes beyond the heart line then the person will stay young at heart and will tackle new and exciting adventures in their later years.

It is rare for the fate line to end under the Jupiter (index) finger, but if it does it may indicate the person is drawn to politics, philosophy or law as their career or area of interest. If the line goes toward the Apollo (ring) finger then the person will excel in creative endeavours such as art, literature, music or design. If the line reaches over to the little finger then the person will be an entertainer or salesperson or be involved in some other career in the communication field.

Mars line

The Mars line, also called the sister line, runs inside and is fainter than the life line and is usually about 1 to 2 cm long. It indicates extra vitality and protection and, according to some palmists, protection from a passed-over relative or animal in spirit. Sometimes it represents extra support for the person in a challenging time of their life.

⊸ Spirit guides ⊷

Cali, a sweet Filipino lady, came in for a reading because her girlfriend had encouraged her to see me. Cali had a Mars line that was about 1.5 cm long that ran parallel to her

life line. She was having a tough time about a big decision in her life, and I told her I felt there was a lady in spirit who was guiding and watching over her. Cali revealed that she had been raised by her aunty because her parents were too poor to bring her up. Cali's aunty was a Buddhist nun who raised Cali in a local temple. Cali told me it had been the most wonderful time of her life and she had many happy memories of those days. Through mediumship I was able to pass on some loving messages from her aunty.

Travel lines

Travel lines are horizontal lines found on the edge of the palm between the wrist and the heart line. Each line is said to represent a trip taken by the person. It is believed the longer and deeper the line, the more important the trip is to the person. Maybe the person took the trip for some sole reason or purpose. The more lines a person has also indicates the level of adventure they may have.

Tune in to the lines and focus on one to see if your superconscious will show you a map or an image to indicate what part of the world they travelled to. Maybe the client did not travel to a place but metaphorically it may mean that the person travelled far and wide in their own life. For example, they may have recovered from a long illness or freed themselves from a difficult or unfulfilling relationship or job.

Line of intuition

The line of intuition or line of Uranus is located on the luna/moon part of the palm and sometimes arcs around or heads towards the mount of Mercury. It is commonly a short line or several short lines 1 to 4 cm long that may go diagonally towards the centre of the palm. The line of intuition symbolises a person who is intuitive and empathic and who may have strong psychic ability. A person with this line could be a medium, healer or psychic and may be drawn to the mystical, paranormal side of life. This person needs to follow their gut feeling as it will help them to navigate their life with more accuracy and higher inner awareness.

Mercury line

The Mercury or health line runs from the bottom of the palm near the wrist up towards the little finger (see the diagram on page 20). It's known to be connected with health issues, although some palmists feel it's more about business expertise and communication skills. I mainly read it as a health line. Sometimes you will spot a Mercury line on a palm but other times there may be only dashes or nothing at all.

A Mercury line that appears strong and deep may indicate health concerns. You will find breaks in the line on most people, which suggests stomach problems, suppressed emotions or a poor diet. Intuitively ask the energy of the line or call on your guides to give you a sense of what's going on for the person you are reading. Recommend the person seek medical help if you are concerned about a health issue. Sometimes if the lines are pale it may mean that the person's health has improved, especially if their past, non-dominant hand has a strong Mercury line yet their future, dominant hand reveals a lighter line. This shows that the person has put focus and energy into their health and therefore it has improved over time.

As a naturopath I love the Mercury line, but it can be a challenge to read so I use my intuition and guides to help gain information on how the client's health is going. Sometimes I will hear a word such as 'water' or see an orange, which usually means the person needs more vitamin C and anti-oxidants such as oranges in their diet.

I was modelling a palmistry reading to my students and asked one of them, Michelle, if I could read her palm. When

I tuned in to her Mercury line I heard the word 'liver' and my gut told me it needed help. Michelle confirmed she had just had a blood test and her liver enzymes were at a bad level. She was cutting back on alcohol and was undertaking other health changes to support her liver health.

Sometimes my third eye (clairvoyance) will show me images of fruit and vegetables or lots of junk food, which guides me as to what to share with the client. I may be shown a plate of meat, which I know means the person needs more protein in their diet so I encourage them to eat more nuts, seeds, legumes and other protein-rich foods.

Wrist lines

Wrist lines are also known as rascettes or bracelet lines. If there are three wrist lines it's called a 'magic bracelet' and is a good luck sign. Some palmists believe rascettes represent travel lines. I sometimes like to relax, breathe deeply, blur my eyes and trance into an alpha state so I can tune in to any messages or images the person's wrists and palms reveal about them; the palms and wrists may energetically share the gifts, abilities and interests a client has. I once saw the image of a paint brush near my client's wrist, and she confirmed she was an artist and was hoping to sell some of her artwork online.

➤ A light along the way ➤

My client, Judith, was 55 years old while her boyfriend was 32. Judith had an infectious laugh and a sunny personality despite enduring a hard life with abusive relationships and the death of her teenage daughter. Her deceased daughter came through via mediumship with loving and accurate messages that Judith found healing and comforting.

Judith deeply loved her younger man but complained that he kept her hidden from family and social events. He never invited her out to gatherings, so she felt as though he didn't respect her or their relationship. Judith had health issues, so we spent a few sessions working on her health, belief patterns and angry feelings towards her partner's family.

Judith sent Scott to see me. He was open to hypnotherapy and reiki so we did several sessions to help his anxiety and relationship concerns. He tearfully shared with me that he yearned for children so his relationship with Judith had to end. On Scott's third session I suggested we look at his palms, on which there were four long relationship lines. He'd had only one relationship prior to the relationship with Judith, and I intuitively sensed there were more relationships to come for him. I suggested to Scott that he be honest and kind to Judith regarding his feelings about their relationship and his plans for the future.

Judith returned the next week and, as I suspected, she mentioned Scott's relationship lines. They had spoken with each other about their relationship and the future of it, and Judith said it was hard for her to accept their relationship may end although she knew in her heart that Scott had become more emotionally disconnected. I asked Judith what she had learned from the relationship, and she replied that she learned that men can be gentle and loving. She talked about what she would do in the future if she had to move on and what type of life she would lead. Judith realised there were many possibilities out there for her, as she had interests and passions she could delve into that would help her to move on with joy and success.

I realised after seeing this couple the power palmistry has to reveal to us things that can help us along our paths in life. It is important to tell clients that palmistry is a light along the way, that there are many probable futures and how you think, act and be will create a path that resonates with your soul.

Sydney line

The Sydney line was discovered in Sydney, Australia and is where the head line stretches right across the hand to the other side of the palm like it's cutting the palm in half. The line may indicate a person who had behavioural and learning difficulties at school. They can be very focused individuals who like to call the shots, have a talent for looking outside the box and a quick mind but can be self-absorbed.

Palm 1   **Palm 2**   **Note:** palm 1 and palm 2 represent 'normal' palms

Simian 1   **Simian 2**   **Simian 3**   **Simian 4**

Sydney 1   **Sydney 2**   **Sydney 3**   **Sydney 4**

Simian line

A simian line or simian crease, where the head and heart lines merge into a single line, are found in 2 to 6 per cent of the population. People with a simian line are energetic and creative and find it challenging to separate their intellect and mind from their heart and emotions. They are also strong, determined and restless and can tend to fly off the handle, so their behaviour can be unpredictable. Their intense concentration means they put their heart and mind into their projects, and if their thumb is short and stiff they can be stubborn.

⟿ Famous people with simian lines ⬿

Well-known people who have simian lines include:

- American actor Robert De Niro, who has one on his left hand
- former British prime minister Tony Blair, who has lines on both hands
- US politician Hillary Clinton, who has one on her left hand.

Formed in the womb by the 12th week and called by some doctors the single palmer crease, the simian line occurs more often in Down syndrome palms. Down syndrome was named by doctor John Down in 1866. In 1906 his son, R.L. Down, discovered the link between the simian line and Down syndrome. The simian line can be linked to other syndromes such as Cohen syndrome, foetal alcohol syndrome or Turner syndrome.

Having a simian line on both hands makes the attributes even more highlighted. Also note that you may see some people with semi-simian (simianesque) lines. A semi-simian line is where there is an extra line splitting or branching off the heart or head line as well as the main joined line.

⤙ Rare lines ⤚

Sydney and simian lines are quite rare to see, so it's interesting when they appear. Once while reading palms at a psychic fair in Canberra several years ago I was excited to read the palm of a lady with a Sydney line and also read the palm of a man with a simian line. What made it even more fascinating for me was when I found out that my own father had a Sydney line! I think he felt quite unique when I informed him it's an unusual line, and it helped me to understand my dad more as he is a successful businessman who likes to have many projects on the go. He is now retired but still likes to connect with others and enjoys the competitive side of lawn bowls.

Exercise 3: *spirit guide and heart meditation*

This exercise will help to develop your skills in connection, perception and intuitive competence, as the more you tune in to your psychic senses the better palm reader you will be. When you open the psychic door to the other realms information will flow more freely, which will help your confidence levels and open up your heart:

- Close your eyes and do the four-step activation sequence (see page 36) to get into a relaxed and intuitive state.

- Breathe in and out of your heart chakra. Imagine you are going deeper and deeper into a restful and happy state.

- Visualise yourself in a serene and magical environment where you feel connected with nature and life. Imagine you are lying down on a comfortable couch in this beautiful place, let go and feel incredible peace, stillness and tranquillity inside you. Breathe deeply.

- Ask your heart and soul what messages they have for you. Relax and wait for any messages, insights, colours, images or feelings to come to you.

- Ask your spirit guide/higher self to communicate with you in a way you will understand and connect with. Relax and wait for any messages, insights, colours, images or feelings to come to you.

- When you are ready, open your eyes and feel the difference in your mind, body and soul!

Chapter 4

Other markings on the palm

'There is a positive side to every marking.'
— John Fincham

While there are palms with no significant markings, some can have one or a combination of marks and features. Keep in mind that some markings can appear or disappear during a lifetime and that different palmistry books have different meanings for the markings, so use your intuition to tap into the meanings.

Islands

Islands are small oval shapes usually found along a line that may indicate a time when there was a challenge to overcome such as an operation or moving house. It could be a period when the person needed to recuperate and take time out to reflect and heal.

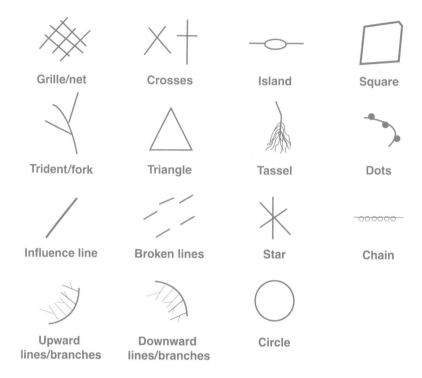

Grille/net   Crosses   Island   Square

Trident/fork   Triangle   Tassel   Dots

Influence line   Broken lines   Star   Chain

Upward
lines/branches   Downward
lines/branches   Circle

Dots

Dots indicate a surprise or an intense event such as a health issue, relationship change or a move. This intense event may create worry, anxiety and tension in a person's life. Recently I read the palm of a 70-year-old man with a deep, red dot on his heart line. I tuned in to the energy of the dot and said: 'I feel there was a time of struggle around the age of 50.' The man replied: 'Yes, that's when I went bankrupt.' Dots, which are usually red or deep pink in colour, mean lessons and growth.

Chains

Chains on a hand indicate a period when someone was occupied with worry, confusion and uneasiness. Maybe the person needs to clear some patterns and beliefs so they can release blocks and see life in a meaningful way, and also to understand that their thoughts and actions create the path ahead. Sometimes challenges are the greatest teachers.

Branches

Branches look like upward and downward lines on the palm. Rising branches are a sign of good fortune and luck, while branches going down towards the wrist may be a sign of frustration. Branches can sometimes represent a person who may have been a friend or a foe. Check what age and time the branches appear along a line and intuit whether it's an event or a person.

Broken lines

Appearing as a gap or split in a line, broken lines represent a shift or change in a person's life that may have made them stop and reflect. Some people experience difficulties in their life such as divorce, illness, death or money issues, but negative experiences usually have a silver lining that make life all the more rich and dynamic. Sometimes the greatest action you can undertake is to forgive and let go; it does take time, but it's worth it. It's good to see people who have moved on in productive and purposeful ways.

Tridents and forks

Forks may indicate a writer's fork or choices, change and opportunity. Tridents at the end of the fate line mean success, a happy life and good fortune.

Circles

Circles, which are rarely found, predict a life of recognition and fortune.

Triangles

Triangles signify a person with great psychic and spiritual abilities who will benefit from harnessing and channelling their innate abilities through classes, books and meditation/yoga practices. Triangles also mean the ability to bounce back and be resilient. I have discovered triangles are portals of energy that link us to the cosmos. Connect with this triangular portal and see if any colours, scenes or images appear with messages for you or your client. See the magic in the triangle!

Squares

Teacher squares mostly appear on the Jupiter mount, but I have also found them on other areas of the palm. Squares highlight that the person has a gift for teaching, writing, healing and counselling, while teacher squares indicate an ability to motivate and inspire others. People who have teacher squares are natural leaders, teachers and managers.

⮞ Teacher squares ⮜

While teaching a palmistry workshop at a local fair I asked for volunteers so I could read some palms. Jill enthusiastically shot her hand up and raced to the front. I held a magnifying glass over her dominant palm and noticed teacher squares on her Jupiter mount, then saw an image of her speaking in front of others. Jill confirmed she had been a school teacher for over 30 years. I also observed teacher squares on her non-dominant hand and said that she was born to be a teacher. Jill laughed and said when she was four years old she told her mother she was going to be a teacher. As a young girl she used to set up mini classrooms with her dolls and her friends in the neighbourhood.

When I had my palm read in my 20s the palm reader asked whether I was a teacher, as I had four teacher squares on my Jupiter mount. The reader was accurate as at the time I was a primary school teacher, then later became a reiki, spiritual and yoga/meditation teacher.

Crosses

Crosses on a line may represent obstacles or blockages along the path that will nevertheless strengthen the person's ability to use their inner and outer resources so they can step forward with courage and determination and achieve their dreams and heart's desires.

Tassels

Although not often seen on hands, tassels can represent scattered energies or ideas that need more concentration and focus.

Grilles and nets

Grilles or nets signify a starting and stopping of movement. A person with a net may need to dig deep into their heart and find out what they really want in life while a grille may indicate a tendency to overdo things, so it is important for people with a grille to slow down and recharge regularly. One palm reader told me that nets and grilles on the Venus mount represent mediumship ability, while others believe a grille on the mount of Venus is a sign of sensuality.

Lines of influence

Small lines about 1 to 2 cm long represent a significant person who comes along at the right place and time and makes a substantial impact on the life of the person with the lines of influence. Even challenging experiences with people can bring great soul awakenings and rewards.

Note that lines of influence can be either someone who is still living or someone who has crossed over. A client in her 30s, Rachael, had a line of influence that went through her life line. I tuned in and felt the line had crossed through her life line at around age 23 and, with tears in her eyes, Rachael revealed her boyfriend Don had died in a car accident when she was 23. I felt Don was still around her, supporting and encouraging her to live her best life.

Stars

Stars are the most fortunate markings on the palm as people with stars usually achieve an amazing accomplishment in their life. They are a good luck sign.

⟿ Good luck stars ⟾

Wendy, a school principal, came to see me for a psychic reading at a big festival in Sydney. I noticed two stars in the middle of her palm near the fate line and told her it was a good luck sign. Wendy smiled and said she'd won a large amount of money in the lottery and had bought a house with the winnings. She pointed to the second star on her hand and exclaimed: 'I have faith that another lot of money will come my way!'

The girdle of Venus

The girdle of Venus starts between the little and ring fingers and runs in a small arc that ends between the Saturn (middle) and Jupiter (index) fingers (see the diagram on page 20). Relating to emotional intelligence, sensuality and touch, it's quite exciting to find although you may not be able to see all of the arc. You will usually only see the beginning and end of the girdle with no line in between.

The girdle of Venus is like a second heart line. Approximately 20 per cent of the people I have seen had the girdle on their palms.

Family chain

A family chain is a line or chain found at the base of the thumb near where the thumb joins the palm. A heavy chain means strong ties to family, while a thin chain means less connection to family and may indicate that the person has decided to step back from their family for various reasons. A break in the line could mean there was a time when the person was less involved with the dynamics of the family and a loose family chain suggests a challenging family relationship.

If you find a darker area on the family chain, tune in to it as you may get a feeling about a challenging relationship for your client around family members such as their mother or father. Healing may be seen in the dominant hand, revealing that changes resolve family issues.

Some palmists believe that two family chains represent two homes or a separation of some sort in the family. While studying palmistry during a trip to India I was taught that the base of the thumb is the love area, and was pleased my intuition had sensed the family chain area at the base of the thumb. After reading many palms you will also start to pick up more meanings from the palms.

Angel path

An angel path will appear in the area between the heart and head lines and look like a landing strip (see the diagram on page 41). A narrow strip reveals a person who is secretive and guarded, a wider strip a broadminded, unconventional and impulsive person. A wide strip can also represent impatience, especially if the head and life lines do not join together at the beginning. Also look to see if the angel paths on each hand are the same or different sizes.

Psychic cross

A psychic cross, which indicates a person with a strong psychic sense, appears in the centre of the angel path area between the head and heart lines (see the diagram on page 41). Each end of a true psychic cross should touch and connect with the head or heart line.

Some palmists call psychic crosses that are floating in the angel path area 'witch and wizard' crosses; they may indicate good intuition and spiritual abilities. I have a psychic cross on my palm.

Mystic cross

One of my palmistry students, Heather, has a mystic cross in the centre of her palm. Although Heather is a professional psychic, she attended my course to become certified in palmistry and to brush up on her skills. Heather's mystic cross is quite striking and looks like a letter 'M' on her palm; she also has long, curved lines of intuition on both of her palms.

A mystic cross reveals a person who is highly intuitive, empathic and very compassionate and who is usually drawn to the spiritual side of life.

Medical stigmata

A medical stigmata is a small patch of vertical lines, usually between four and six, beneath the little finger on the Mercury mount (see the diagram on page 41). Medical stigmata are seen on people who are healers, nurses, hypnotherapists, naturopaths or counsellors. I did a palmistry reading for a lady with a medical stigmata on her Mercury mount and told her this indicated she would excel in healing and the medical profession. She said: 'Spot on, I'm a nurse!' Twenty to 30 per cent of the population will have a medical stigmata.

St Andrew's Cross

A St Andrew's Cross will be found on the hands of people who have saved the life of another. I did a palm reading for Sara and noticed she had a St Andrew's Cross on her dominant right hand near the luna or moon mount area of her palm. Sara had a friend who told her she had saved their life because her friendship and support stopped the friend from committing suicide.

Percussion

The percussion area of the palm exists below the Mercury (little) finger and goes right down to the wrist area. I remember it as the part of the hand you use whenever you do a karate chop!

Fine lines

Many fine, spidery lines on a palm will appear for people who are very sensitive and empathic. As they pick up and absorb other people's emotions it can make them feel anxious, so they need to learn to discern between their own and others' feelings and not take on the concerns of others as it can be very draining.

Chapter 5
The fingers

Phalanges (singular 'phalanx') are the bones of the fingers and toes. Each finger has three phalanges and three external sections or segments, although I have seen some people with four. The tip of a finger represents the mind, the middle section represents the body and the bottom section represents the soul or spirit. I have read palmistry books that state the thumb has three sections, but medical dictionaries record the thumb as having just two. The thumb is classified as the first digit (finger) of the hand; its tip signifies willpower while the bottom section represents logic and common sense.

In palmistry, astronomical words are used to name each finger. The index finger is called Jupiter, the middle finger is Saturn, the ring finger is Apollo or sun and the pinky finger is known as Mercury.

The Mercury finger is connected to the heart, energy and love; the sun finger is about releasing and transformation; the Saturn finger is about circulation and kundalini; the Jupiter finger is about intestines and letting go; and the thumb is about lungs and emotions.

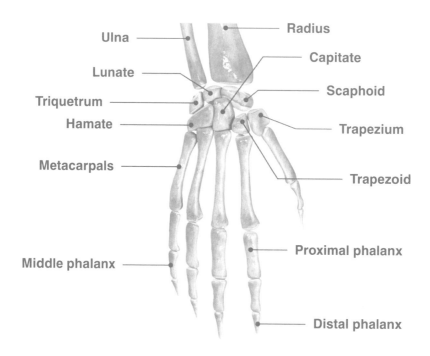

Fingers	What they represent
Mercury: little finger	Ability to communicate, speak, act, write, connect
Apollo/sun: ring finger	Creativity, artistic ability, outlook, abundance, relationships

Saturn: middle finger	Responsibility, reliability, business, reflection, values
Jupiter: index finger	Leadership, ambition, desire to develop and succeed
Chiron: thumb	Personality, character, expression in the world, drive, influence, confidence

⌐ Nadine's four segments ⌐

Nadine, a lady I once read for, had four segments on her Saturn (middle) finger even though she had the same number of joints that other people have. I tuned in to the meaning of this and felt the extra section meant she had more confidence and responsibility in her life. Nadine tended to assume a lot of responsibility, and was enabling others by doing for them what they could do for themselves. Instead of over-caring for others, Nadine needed to model and teach others through her actions and appropriate self-care and self-responsibility. She said she wanted to take time out to go within to find more peace and happiness.

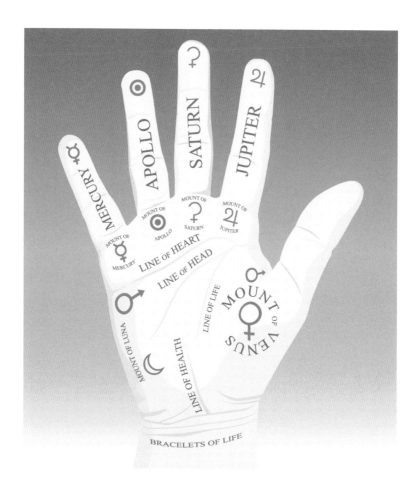

Finger lengths

The index finger, Jupiter, should ideally reach halfway up the top section of the Saturn (middle) finger. If the Jupiter finger is long it may signify ambition, flexibility and charisma. It also means the person has managerial and leadership abilities but that they need to keep their ego in check and lead with compassion and a kind heart. Good

leaders practise what they preach. If the Jupiter finger is longer than the sun (ring) finger it may mean the person is self-focused, optimistic and an inspirational leader. A longer Jupiter finger gives more strength to the thumb.

A short Jupiter finger may mean a lack of drive, motivation and focus, relationships that need repair and healing and low self-esteem, particularly if the head and heart lines are joined. People with a short Jupiter finger would benefit from visualisations, a positive belief in their own talents and skills and perhaps from seeing a coach or doing courses around time management so they can strive forward with more impetus and inner power in their life.

If the Jupiter and sun finger are the same length it represents balance and good self-esteem. A straight Jupiter finger indicates a secure person. If the Jupiter finger bends towards the Saturn finger it may represent a jealous and envious nature. This envy can sometimes propel a person to do better, especially if the energy is used in a productive and useful way. Be careful to check whether the bent finger has come from an injury or arthritis, as those things can cause some people to have curved fingers.

The Saturn or middle finger is about how responsible and social people are. This centre finger highlights how a person's inner strength leads them to creating a life with leadership, power and success, to attain what they think they are worthy of. Some palmists believe that people prone to mental health issues may have their Jupiter and Saturn fingers the same length, so check if mental health concerns run in the family and what steps the person is taking to keep their mental health on track. If the Saturn finger is short the person needs to learn about responsibility in life and how to speak their truth, and they need to follow through on their word and act with integrity. If the Saturn finger is the same length as the sun or Jupiter finger it could indicate a person who procrastinates and lacks belief in their ability to succeed. Past generations may have had challenges, so this finger could highlight the need to overcome insecurities, rise to challenges and heal past and present karma. By healing and releasing the past with love it allows you to have more freedom and energy to live your life's true purpose.

The Apollo or sun finger represents love, beauty, happiness, security and the desire for peace and romance. It can also reflect a person's level of self-esteem and their creativity and subconscious.

The Mercury or pinky finger reflects communication abilities through talking and writing. A long little finger signifies a good lover, especially if the heart line is curved and heads towards the Jupiter mount, because you need good communication skills to enrapture your lover and open their heart and soul. A long Mercury finger may also indicate above-average writing ability and communication skills along with independence. These people are creative souls who like doing things based on their intuition and inner intelligence.

A shorter Mercury finger may denote that the person does not express themselves well and that they're not as comfortable as others socially. This person may need to learn how to communicate well and ask for what they need from self and others, as bottling up emotions may cause health issues. A thick Mercury finger means the person is good at a job where there is a lot of talking, as this person likes to share their opinion and knowledge.

Fingertip shapes

You may find a combination of fingertip shapes on some hands.

Square fingertips

People with square fingertips are practical and down-to-earth and like to do things methodically. They may be

conventional and conservative so may need to become adventurous and do things outside their comfort zone.

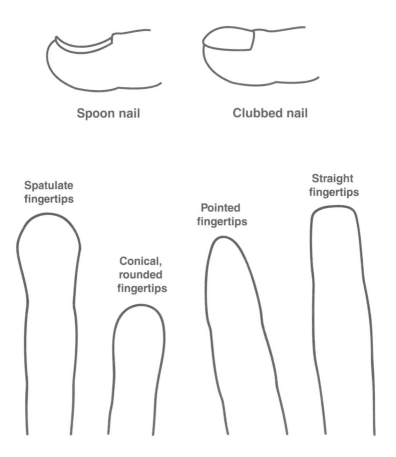

Spoon nail   Clubbed nail

Spatulate fingertips

Conical, rounded fingertips

Pointed fingertips

Straight fingertips

Spatulate fingertips

People with spatulate fingertips are rational and have a realistic approach to life. They enjoy travel and the outdoors and live active, energetic lifestyles, so they need to learn to slow down and smell the roses.

Pointed fingertips

Pointed fingertips appear on people who are thoughtful, intelligent and flexible in life. They love interacting with other people and enjoy good conversation. They are creative, excel at practical endeavours and are drawn to the mystical side of life.

Conical, rounded fingertips

People with conical fingertips enjoy beauty and serenity. They can be idealistic and are visionaries, think on their feet and are fast at assessing situations. They have strong beliefs but need to be careful with their emotions and learn to appropriately master how they express themselves.

Straight fingertips

People with straight fingertips are frank, honest, diligent, energetic and impulsive. They think clearly and like to achieve, and usually know how to express their feelings.

Knotty fingers

In these cases, if you turn the finger and look at it side on you will see bumps where the joints of the fingers are, and if you touch the joint you will be able to feel the bumpy bone on the finger. Knotty fingers are linked to people

who are educated and are professor types who like to study and take in facts in minute detail. These people are very organised and plan every move they make, and may not like spontaneity as much as others do as they like to plot and plan and make sure every detailed is covered. This can make them feel uptight and seem controlling but, as these people grow older, they learn to let go more, be present and go with the flow.

Rings on fingers

Before a reading with a palm reader many years ago I was preparing to take my rings off when he said: 'Leave your rings on, as it's important I see which fingers have rings on them.' This is what is indicated by the wearing of rings on particular fingers:

- Wearing a ring on the Jupiter (index) finger means you like being a leader and taking the initiative.
- Wearing a ring on the Saturn (middle) finger shows that you enjoy standing out from the crowd and being social.
- Wearing a ring on the Apollo/sun (ring) finger shows that you have an open heart. You like to get

along with others and have an affinity with animals and children.

- Wearing a ring on the Mercury (little) finger reveals a determination to succeed and to progress through life with focus and dedication.
- A ring worn on the thumb shows a person who is creative and outspoken and who thinks outside the box.

Oestrogen and testerone levels

I love interesting and burgeoning scientific facts, as do many of my students. One of them is that the second and fourth fingers reveal a person's oestrogen and testosterone levels. It is known as the 2D:4D ratio, stemming from the fact that the index finger is the second digit (starting from the thumb as number one) and the ring finger is the fourth digit. Scientists measure the length of the second finger (2D) and divide it by the length of the fourth finger (4D) to gauge the levels of oestrogen and testosterone.

Men typically have a longer ring finger and women a longer index finger, because the fourth finger is linked to testosterone and the second finger to oestrogen. Men have 10 to 20 times more testosterone in their bodies than women, but the levels decline by about 1 per cent each year after the age of 30. A study that compared the 2D:4D ratio and looked into the habits of men and women discovered that the longer your ring finger is when compared with your index finger, the higher levels of testosterone you were exposed to in the womb and then the more likely you were to engage in sexual activity. Yet the research professors also explained that human behaviour is affected by many factors, that what happened in the womb has only a minor effect on sexual and mating habits (https://phys.org/news/2015-02-stray-delves-sexual-behaviour.html).

Exercise 4: *finger spread*

Shake your hands and then rest them in mid-air in front of you with your palms facing you. Take note of how your fingers are spread out:

- Hands held with all the fingers spread apart reveal a person who enjoys life and is friendly and outgoing and likes creative adventures.
- Hands with fingers held close together or cupped reveal a person who is shy and tends to procrastinate.
- A space between Mercury and Apollo reveals a person who is independent and needs lots of freedom and space.
- A space between Apollo and Saturn reveals a person who may be single-minded and very focused.
- A space between Saturn and Jupiter reveals a person who likes to lead and likes to have projects and plans on the go.
- Saturn and Apollo together signify a creative person who thinks outside the box.

Chapter 6

The thumb

The thumb is situated next to the index or Jupiter finger. It has just two sections (and two bones), while the fingers have three sections and bones each. The longer and stronger the thumb is the more the person will complete in their lifetime. The tip of the thumb near the nail reflects your willpower, and the lower part of the thumb is your logic area.

Chiron was a centaur in Greek mythology who was a healer and teacher; Chiron is the name by which I call the thumb, as it is the healer inside all of us! It represents our deepest spiritual wounds and our efforts to heal those wounds and can therefore be considered to be a wounded healer and teacher. When I studied palmistry in India I learned that they call the thumb 'Venus', which makes sense as the Venus mound is below the thumb.

The thumb, a barometer of how much you will accomplish in this lifetime, is a healing digit with the power to inspire and create strength and healing. It is a commanding finger as it helps us to both physically and metaphorically grip and hold things. How well do you have a grip on your life?

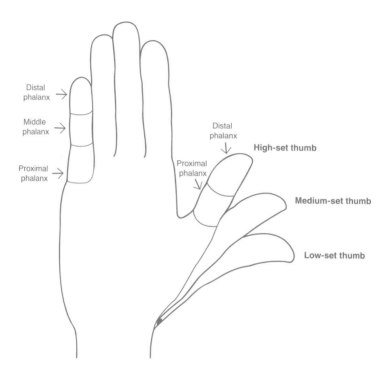

Thumb setting

When the whole hand is opened out the thumb sometimes has a 90-degree or L-shaped angle, to the index finger, which is called a low-set thumb. An individual with a low-set thumb is quite open, reliable, trustworthy, adaptable, flexible, independent and social.

A high-set thumb is less than a 90-degree angle when the hand is opened out and indicates a careful, conservative person with a fear of letting go.

A medium-set thumb indicates a person who is creative, thoughtful and focused.

⟿ Self-doubt and low self-esteem ⟾

I had known Lucy for many years; she was 72 years young and had very short, high-set thumbs. A high-set thumb indicates a person who does not stand up for themselves and may need encouragement to speak their truth and to believe they are valuable and have something important to say. Lucy had struggled all her life with self-doubt and low self-esteem. In this lifetime her lessons were to learn self-confidence, positive thinking and to not be a victim. She realised her recurring self-sabotaging patterns and went on to find pleasure in volunteer work, becoming better at communicating her needs to others. It's an ongoing process, but Lucy is finding more happiness in her life and is taking her power back!

Thumb shapes

A square-tipped thumb represents business and projects. A clubbed thumb is a genetic trait whereby the end of the thumb is short and round and the nail bed is short and wide. A clubbed thumb represents a person who is traditional, shy and tense and who bottles up their feelings, and also a person who can be fiery, which may cause a rise in their blood pressure.

Angela is a smart 31-year-old real estate agent with clubbed thumbs on both hands. I tuned in to her health line and felt she had reflux; she confirmed she was taking medicine for acid reflux. Angela was finding it hard to accept her ex-boyfriend had dumped her two years ago. Energetically, acid reflux is about not digesting life, being irritated about what is happening and feeling helpless in life. Angela's emotions were bubbling up inside her, so healing her feelings about her ex-partner would help her to calm down her anxiety and bring resolution to the situation.

A thumb that is held close to the side of the hand shows a penny-pinching person.

A thumb that sticks out indicates a carefree personality.

A short thumb signifies a lack of confidence and low self-esteem.

People with a lower thumb joint that is prominent and pokes out may have musical ability.

Large thumbs indicate a stronger personality, while small thumbs show that the person is gentler. Long, broad thumbs belong to people who push hard and succeed. People who want to succeed but need more focus and driving force have long, narrow thumbs. Small, broad thumbs are on people who lack determination, and thumbs with an exceptionally wide top belong to more aggressive people. A thick top joint shows a person who may be blunt and straight to the point, while a tapered tip shows a person who has subtle ways of doing things.

The shape of the thumb's tip is a strong indicator of inner power. A pointed or conical thumb indicates an impulsive, perceptive nature, while a square thumb is a sign of common sense. A bulbous tip may indicate a bad temper, and a tip that bends far back shows a person who is artistic or involved in an unusual interest or occupation. A person with a flat-tipped thumb is impatient and full of nervous energy.

Will and logic

The top part of the thumb is known as the 'will' area, while the bottom part is the 'logic' area. Will indicates a person's drive and how they apply that in their life. Logic represents their ability to reason and make sensible, rational decisions. If the logic part of the thumb is longer the person talks more than they act, so they need to put their hopes and dreams into action.

If the will part of the thumb is the smaller part it indicates a nervous, energetic person. If the will area is longer the person may be impulsive and needs to think before they leap. People with a longer will section of the thumb are also quite strong-willed, determined and to the point, which will work well if they learn to channel these traits in the right direction. It's even better if they have a long Mercury (little) finger, which indicates they know how to communicate their needs and have compassion when interacting with others.

People whose logic part of their thumb is longer have a black and white approach and a common-sense brain, which means they sum up situations well. If this person's logic combines with good intuition it enables them to make choices from both their logical left brain and their intuitive right brain. A person who only comes from logic and ego makes for a hard-headed person who finds relationships difficult, as their heart chakra may be closed from pain, sadness or blocks. Part of their life's journey is to feel love and to express their needs to self and others.

Some people have similar-sized thumb segments, meaning the will and logic areas are quite well balanced. A person with a large logic segment would do well with meditation to activate the right intuitive brain, while a person with a big will area would do well to set goals so they keep focused on their dreams in life.

Supple and stiff thumbs

A thumb that curves back into a bend or curl is called a supple, flexible thumb. People with this type of thumb are easygoing, versatile, emotional, have compassion for

Stiff thumb   **Supple/flexible thumb**

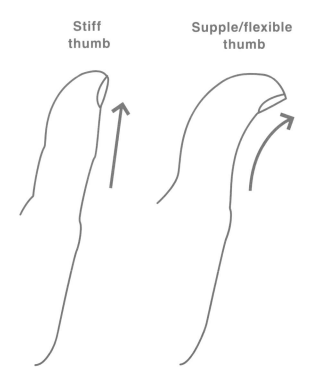

others and enjoy giving, although they can be too generous with money and may overspend. They achieve success through bouts of brilliance that build up to create a life of passion and devotion. People with a supple, flexible thumb like to lead the way but can also be good followers.

A stiff thumb doesn't bend back like the supple, flexible thumb. People with a straighter thumb are practical, have common sense and look at all sides before making a decision. They can be cautious with their money and are good savers. Stiff-thumbed people can be stubborn, yet they can learn to roll along with the ebbs and flows of life.

Exercise 5: *thumb cross exercise*

Shake your hands for a few seconds. Breathe in and out and relax.

Clasp your hands together and notice which thumb is on top when you cross your hands over each other.

If the right thumb ends up on top it reveals that the left side of your brain dominates so you tend to be more analytical and logical. You enjoy planning and plotting, and would benefit from doing meditation and visualisation

exercises to open up your right brain so you can tap into your intuitive and creative powers and help your life flow abundantly.

If the left thumb remains on top the right side of your brain dominates. You are a more creative and intuitive type who uses logic with a blend of intuition, but you need to remember to stay on task and keep focused so you can achieve your goals. Balancing the left and right brain, with careful planning and your creative flair, will help to create a successful life.

Chapter 7

The nails and the mounts

It takes approximately six months for a fingernail to grow. If the nails are brittle and often break it may indicate the person has nutrition and absorption problems. Broken nails can also be caused by the products used to paint nails, so be aware this can affect nail quality. Yellow nails or skin may relate to liver issues or beta carotene, which is the red-orange colour found in fruits and vegetables. If someone has been eating a lot of carrots their skin and nails may be yellowish.

Clubbing nails

Clubbing nails are where nails curve down over the fingertips, which may be caused by low oxygen levels in the blood and could be a sign of lung, liver or bowel issues.

Spoon nails

Spoon nails are concave shaped and could indicate an iron deficiency.

Nail and hand health

You may notice white spots on a person's nails. Naturopaths believe that four or more white spots on a nail suggest low zinc levels in the body. A 54-year-old client, Glen, had around five to seven white spots on several of his nails, so I suggested he could have low zinc levels and a resultingly poor immune system, as zinc helps with immunity. Glen confirmed he had been unwell, so I suggested he eat more zinc-rich foods such as pumpkin seeds, seafood and spinach. Low zinc levels may also suggest an individual is going through a period of stress. A poor diet of too much sugar, wheat, junk food and alcohol can deplete the good minerals such as zinc in the body.

If the hands appear a bit shaky it could indicate magnesium deficiency or other health concerns. Suggest your client see a health-care practitioner to further investigate their health.

Warts on a hand may represent a virus and thus, energetically, a person who feels powerless in some area of their life. Some warts remain dormant and are flat on the skin, but when active a wart will rise up on the hand. Find which location on the fingers or palm the wart appears and see what it represents for your client. My client Kelly had a raised wart at the base of her Jupiter (index) finger on the proximal phalanx, which indicated Kelly had fears about standing in her own truth and being a leader in her career. She did some self-reflection and meditations to heal her subconscious and clear any outdated beliefs she had.

As a naturopath I find the health side of the hands fascinating. I don't always look at the back of the hands, but sometimes I feel drawn to turning hands over and viewing the nails. One male I saw at a psychic fair had a prominent red colour around the skin near the base of his nails. Redness can indicate candida or an issue with gut health, so I discussed with him the importance of hydration and the ingestion of fresh fruit and vegetables to help clean out his intestines. He agreed he had been eating a lot of processed foods and needed to clean up his diet. I also read for a lovely nurse who had vertical ridges on all her nails. Vertical ridges may mean the person is not absorbing nutrients well.

Looking at a client's nails helps me to assess the person's body and overall health. Of course, if they are wearing nail polish it can be a challenge!

Onychomancy

Onychomancy is a form of divination performed through the fingernails. Some cultures look at the shape, colours or marks on the nails to interpret their insights and predictions. The base of the nail represents the future, the middle of the nail is the present and the top of the nail is the past. A white spot on the:

- thumb may mean a present or gift
- index finger can indicate a kind and generous person
- middle finger says to be cautious and make wise choices
- ring finger indicates a new venture or relationship
- little finger shows that travel or a trip is on the horizon.

Mounts

Traditionally, mounts are the areas under each finger, or zone, of the palm, yet I find they sometimes appear in between these areas. The mounts reveal a person's energy and talents. If you feel the bones under the mounts you may be able to gauge the size and energy of each mount; also, feeling the mounts helps to connect with the energy of them. Sometimes I'm drawn to reading the mounts

or I may focus on a mount that stands out to me. The following information will help you when studying the dynamics of the mounts on the hand, but you should also use your intuition to guide you.

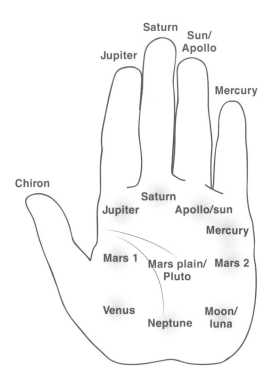

The mount of Jupiter

The Jupiter mount is found at the base of the index finger. A puffy, rounded mount shows a person's leadership abilities, honesty, optimism and love of socialising. If the mount is flat the person may lack confidence and drive to succeed, so look at healing any unhelpful beliefs or family patterns.

Teacher squares that are joined together so they look like a ladder may be found on the Jupiter mount (and also on the Mars plain); this is known as a ladder of success and indicates the person will attain their goals and aspirations.

The mount of Saturn

The Saturn mount is situated at the base of the middle finger. If it is well developed the person is responsible and is a wisdom seeker. If the mount is flat the person is driven and succeeds if focused enough. You may find the Saturn mount is naturally a bit flat.

A triangle on the mount of Saturn shows psychic ability.

The mount of Apollo

The Apollo or sun mount is at the base of the ring finger. If it is plump the person is warm and enthusiastic. If it is flat the person needs to learn gratitude, because when they appreciate life more goodness will come to them as their heart and mind will be open to new possibilities and abundance.

A star on the Apollo mount is a very good sign that indicates wealth and prestige, while a triangle indicates good luck. A circle is very rare and indicates fame.

The mount of Mercury

The Mercury mount is situated at the base of the little finger and symbolises our ability to communicate and interact with others. A well-formed mount shows a person who enjoys travel and is vibrant and vivacious. If the mount is flat the person may be shy and needs to learn to speak up in life. A developed, rounded mount signifies an effective communicator who is good at business and in the corporate world.

A star on the mount of Mercury indicates a successful career. A triangle shows someone who gets on well with other people. A grille may indicate a nervous, empathic person with a sensitive soul who tunes in to the energy of others easily.

The moon mount

The moon or luna mount is situated at the base of the palm opposite the thumb and under the little finger, but right down near the wrist area. The luna mount represents imagination, subconscious and intuition. A well-developed moon mount is a sign of good psychic ability, while a healthy, rounded mount shows a person who is compassionate, caring and passionate about life. Even if the mount is flat it's still a positive sign, as it shows a person who is imaginative, compassionate and, like the moon, tuned in to their emotions and intuitive side.

A star on the mount of the moon shows someone with a strong imagination.

The mount of Venus

The Venus mount is found under the base of the thumb. If the Venus mount is well developed the person is warm, generous and kind-hearted and will be a good friend and listener. If the mount is flat it may reveal the person is lethargic and needs to recharge their batteries. Ask the person what they are drinking, as a flat mount is linked to dehydration. The Venus mount is related to the kidney area of the hand. Coffee and alcohol dehydrate the body, so the person needs to be aware they need to give their body hydrating foods such as fruit, vegetables and herbal teas. They might also benefit from cutting down on acidic foods such as sugar and wheat as well as learning to control acidic negative thoughts.

A cross on the mount of Venus indicates a person who will find true love in their lifetime. A square means protection around love.

The mount of Neptune

The Neptune mount is at the middle bottom of the hand near the wrist. A developed, rounded mount indicates a charming, magnetic person who likes performing.

A circle or triangle on the mount of Neptune indicates great artistic and musical talent.

Mars 1 (positive)

Mars 1 is positioned between the thumb and index finger and indicates courage and following beliefs. There are usually folds of skin in this area. Tune in to the energy of this part of the palm, which some palmists link to father energy, as it may indicate how many mountains have to be conquered to achieve peace and harmony.

Mars 2 (negative)

Mars 2 is found under the Mercury (little) finger below the heart line. It represents how committed a person is to social and community-based causes.

Mars plain (mount of Pluto)

The Mars plain or mount of Pluto is located in the centre of the palm in between Mars 1 and 2. I feel the Mars plain represents the true heart and soul of a person as the centre part of the palm is like a portal of energy. It represents the 11th chakra of the body, along with the soles of the feet. This chakra is coloured pink and helps you both receive and release energy from your body. If you do not clear other people's energy you can feel a heaviness around your feet and body.

Years ago after seeing clients I would sometimes feel a heavy energy around my feet, and I realised I needed to clear my energy field. Meditating before I see clients and being in nature helps my body to release and clear my energy field. At the end of the day it's wonderful to feel grateful and to wish the very best for clients and their journey ahead.

Tune in to the Mars plain and see what you intuitively pick up on in this area. Ask the person's higher self/soul to communicate with you and provide information that will help your client on their path.

Many fine lines on the plain of Mars show a person with an anxious temperament who may have an empathic nature. A cross shows a person who tends to be outspoken and candid about their views. A triangle or grille on this mount indicates strong psychic powers.

Summary of the mounts

Jupiter	Signifies ambition, enthusiasm and how a person socialises.
Saturn	Symbolises responsibility, stability and time-management abilities.
Apollo or sun	Represents love of life, spontaneity, productivity, creativity and success.
Mercury	Represents wisdom, study, intelligence and resilience.
Moon or luna	Represents intuition, imagination and emotions.
Venus	Represents passion, sensuality and touch.
Neptune	Linked to music, art and spirituality.

Chapter 8

Scrying and the mind

Scrying is a technique whereby you stare or gaze as though in a trance into a medium such as water or metal or smoke in order to get messages or meanings. It may also be called 'crystal gazing'. A sacred art that has been used in many cultures, scrying can reveal the past, present and future but is a skill that requires practice, faith and devotion.

I encourage people to de-focus, to soften their gaze and see what their third eye reveals to them. My own scrying has developed over the years: I switch from my physical eye to my third eye and allow the higher realms to show me what I need to know. We are all gifted with an inner eye; welcome its presence in your life and be surprised by its wisdom and connection with you.

I love to use scrying when I'm doing palmistry or giving psychic readings as it allows me to tap in to the energy of the person and gives me pertinent information. I learned scrying many years ago at a psychic and meditation class I attended. The teacher placed several crystal balls around the room and taught us how to scry by using our psychic senses; she also showed us how to scry on a mirror and a door. During the class I looked into a crystal ball and saw a symbolic image of a forest with galloping horses running among the trees, which was exciting for me to see as it reflected what was happening in my life at the time.

Some people scry with their eyes open while others do so with closed eyes. To one student's question about whether images come into your mind's eye or outside of it I replied that some people are stronger in one method or the other, so you should see which works best for you.

Visualisation practice

This awakening activity will take you into that realm where all good palmists and psychics go:

- Start by seeing the images and symbols, so when you connect with the higher realms you are able to recognise the language of the spiritual realm.
- Imagine a vibrant green apple with a smiley face on it.

- Where do you see that image: is the apple suspended in space in front of you or inside your head and third eye area?
- Maybe you do not see a picture but you sense it in some other way. Take note and practise more. For example, imagine a flower or imagine yourself on your bed. Be aware of your senses and how your mind forms these images for you.
- Journal your experiences and see how they evolve with practice. Good luck!

The mind

In palmistry your mind helps you to focus and be of service to clients. If you are scattered and restless it will affect the way you read palms and the energy you bring to this sacred art. Your brain and its waves of energy are intriguing, as your actions can affect them both greatly. Many people have a fast mind that jumps around from one thing to the next in a restless way – known as a 'monkey mind' – and doing yoga and regular meditations can help the monkey slow down. I have noticed my own brain waves have altered due to meditation and yoga, which has helped me to better tune in as a psychic and to tap into different energy frequencies. Being in nature is also an effective way to be in harmony with your heart and mind.

> Understanding the different ways in which the brain and mind work will help you to harness your mind and consciousness in a way that will surprise you and your clients.

The *conscious* mind includes short-term memory and your ability to plan and think critically. The *subconscious* mind involves long-term memories and emotions and your habits, patterns and creativity. The *superconscious* mind is universal wisdom, which is believed to hold all knowledge.

How powerful is your subconscious mind?

According to development biologist Bruce Lipton the subconscious is a processor that is a million times more powerful than our conscious mind (*The Honeymoon Effect*, p. 75, Hay House, USA). The subconscious mind processes in images and emotions, so our thoughts and feelings are vital to tapping into this area of our brain. That's why visualisations and meditations are effective, as they imprint information into your subconscious and help to break patterns and beliefs that are no longer useful.

The superconscious mind is the part that goes beyond your consciousness into a realm of all-knowing and all-being where wisdom and insight exist. When you go into deeper states of being you can tap into this vast warehouse of data to find out what makes ourselves and others tick.

Scientists now say the brain can rewire itself, which is known as neuroplasticity. I love to tell clients about this as it means our brains can change with good choices. A brain functions best with enjoyable exercise, fun hobbies, sleep, low stress levels and nutritious food. It's important to tell your clients they have the power to change the way their brain is wired as this can affect their life in positive and purposeful ways.

Brain waves

Understanding your brain's patterns will make you better able to connect with your mind and its thoughts: when you're relaxing your brain goes into alpha mode; when you're busy your beta mind is doing its job; and when you are healing you are in theta mode or deeper. I found the sessions I undertook with my clients improved when I did exercises to help me go into deeper brain waves. Your palmistry sessions will be more effective when you understand that you have so much power to affect how your mind moves – like a beautiful ocean wave that undulates in the moonlight.

Human brain waves

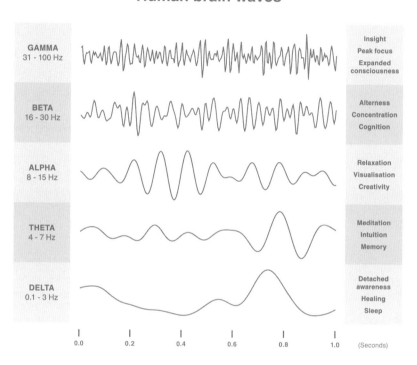

Beta	Beta waves include your conscious thoughts and logical thinking. You are in a beta state when you read, write and socialise with others. Beta waves are good for memory and problem solving.

Alpha	Alpha waves link between conscious thinking and the subconscious mind. Meditation and yoga can put you into an alpha state.
Theta	Theta waves occur during sleep and daydreaming and indicate a deeply relaxed state. They tap into the subconscious and beyond.
Delta	Delta waves are the slowest recorded brain waves, affecting unconscious areas such as heartbeat and digestion. Delta waves include your dreams, astral travel and deep healing and are linked to the superconscious.
Gamma	Gamma waves are important for learning, memory and information processing. It is believed gamma waves tap into the superconscious.

The importance of breathing deeply

Did you know that 10 deep, slow breaths help to get you into a more receptive and relaxed state? As you are reading this you will most likely be in beta brain waves. After 10 deep breaths (or another relaxation method) you will most likely drop into an alpha brain wave state. If you go even deeper you will be in the theta brain wave level.

Exercise 6: *how to scry*

- Begin with the four-step activation sequence (see page 36) to help you tune in to and shift your brain wave energy and vibration. The more you do these four steps the quicker the process will become and the more you will notice the benefits.

- When you are tuned in, look at both of your palms and connect with their energy by blurring your eyes and seeing if any colours, images, scenes, words or feelings come to you. This is scrying.

- Ask your hands what messages they have for you: you may be surprised by what you find! Allow your intuition and guide to help, relaxing and allowing it to come to you. The more you relax beforehand and breathe deeply the more you will receive, as you will be putting your brain into an alpha/theta state where the subconscious and superconscious realms are.

- Repeat these steps: the more you do them the better you will be able to tune in.

Have fun and practise on willing friends and family members. Keep practising and ask your guides and the superconscience to help you receive appropriate and useful information.

Note: if I see an image such as a beach around a client's palms it could indicate they are soon to go on a holiday or that they need to relax and take time out for themselves. Ask the image to tell you more if you require more clarity about what it symbolises. Use a dream dictionary to help you identify symbols if you wish to.

Advanced exercise

Try scrying a flower or an animal and feeling the energy and presence that emanates from them. Do they have a message for you? Merge with their energy and tune in to the vibrations.

Chapter 9

Reflexology and the meridians

Reflexology is based on the Chinese belief that certain areas on the feet or hands have reflex zones that consist of millions of nerve endings linked to other parts of the body. For 3,000 years the Chinese have massaged hands and feet with pressure on certain points that promote good health and well-being to stimulate organs, nerve endings and energy pathways.

You may want to massage or press areas of your own hands to understand the different sensations and feelings particular areas of your hands have. Close your eyes while doing this and notice if any areas are tender. Sometimes the adrenal gland, situated near the life line, may be tight and tender and indicate the need to rest and recharge.

Hand reflexology chart

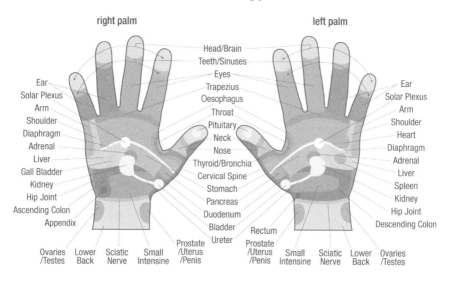

right palm

left palm

Head/Brain
Teeth/Sinuses
Eyes
Trapezius
Oesophagus
Throat
Pituitary
Neck
Nose
Thyroid/Bronchia
Cervical Spine
Stomach
Pancreas
Duodenum
Bladder
Ureter
Rectum

Ear
Solar Plexus
Arm
Shoulder
Diaphragm
Adrenal
Liver
Gall Bladder
Kidney
Hip Joint
Ascending Colon
Appendix

Ear
Solar Plexus
Arm
Shoulder
Heart
Diaphragm
Adrenal
Liver
Spleen
Kidney
Hip Joint
Descending Colon

Ovaries
/Testes

Lower
Back

Sciatic
Nerve

Small
Intensine

Prostate
/Uterus
/Penis

Prostate
/Uterus
/Penis

Small
Intensine

Sciatic
Nerve

Lower
Back

Ovaries
/Testes

I studied reflexology many years ago and am a qualified massage therapist. Through learning these modalities I became more aware of the clever design of our bodies. I incorporated hand reflexology information into my palmistry courses and the students were amazed by how much reflexology tied in with palmistry.

The Venus mount is linked to the pancreas and bladder. A flat Venus may mean low energy and vitality and dehydration, as the pancreas is concerned with the sweetness of life while the bladder represents fluid and proper hydration. People with a flat Venus mount need to rest and balance their lives extra carefully, and you may wish to recommend to your clients that they drink more water or herbal teas. The body is made up of 75 to 80 per cent water, which the organs and brain need a lot of so the cells function well. You will find that you read palms better when you are well watered and fed yourself! It is important to remind people that caffeine drinks are diuretics that take water out of the body.

In reflexology the small intestine is at the bottom of the palm on the Neptune mount, where the via lascivia (line of allergy) usually appears. The small intestine is where you digest and absorb your food, so this line reveals allergies and intolerances.

Your right hand is linked with the liver because your liver is situated on the right-hand side of your body, under your ribs. In reflexology, the arm and shoulder area of the hand is represented under the pinky finger and relates to relationships. How do you shoulder your relationships? What relationship burdens do you carry on your shoulders? How do your arms extend out to others: openly, or with arms crossed?

Meridians

Meridians are energetic channels of invisible energy lines that run life force energy through your body.

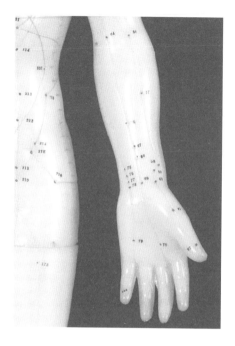

I studied meridians many years ago while learning kinesiology and noticed the meridians mentioned below were linked with particular fingers.

The **heart** meridian ends at the tip of the Mercury (little) finger:

- If imbalanced a person will experience shortness of breath, palpitations, poor memory and sleep, sadness, depression, anxiety, fear and jealousy.
- If balanced a person will experience serenity, love, positivity, happiness and vitality.

The **triple warmer** meridian begins at the Apollo (ring) finger on the outside corner of the nail:

- If imbalanced a person will feel out of sorts and lethargic.
- If balanced a person will experience joy and kindness.

The **sex (circulation)** meridian ends at the tip of the Saturn (middle) finger:

- If imbalanced a person will have health issues around the heart, head and stomach, will experience fears and have poor communication skills.
- If balanced a person will have healthy relationships and experience joy and contentment.

The **large intestine** meridian starts at the end of the Jupiter (index) finger:

- If imbalanced a person will have congested lungs, sluggish bowels and cramps and experience sadness, grief and worry.
- If balanced a person will have good self-esteem and motivation and be relaxed.

The **lung** meridian ends at the tip of the thumb:

- If imbalanced a person will experience despair, sadness and grief.
- If balanced a person will have high self-esteem and self-respect and be honest.

Exercise 7: *palm-healing tap*

Tapping exercises activate the meridian points, and you can tap the fingertips to stimulate them. Close your eyes while doing it and breathe deeply. Affirm quietly to yourself what your heart and soul need at this present time and then observe the difference in the way it makes you feel. You may notice changes over several days. Your intention and ability to rest and rejuvenate are powerful for your spirit and body.

One day I felt a bit congested in my lungs and blocked in my sinuses. I tapped all of my fingertips, especially my thumb which is the lung meridian. While tapping my fingers I asked for healing, grace and peace to come into my life; I sensed higher beings and my guide around me. I lay down for five minutes while I rested my palms on my body, and allowed my body's natural healing response to take place while I relaxed and breathed deeply. My nose and lungs felt clearer within 10 minutes. It's amazing how something so simple can be so effective.

These are the palm healing steps:

- Lie or sit in a comfortable position. Close your eyes and allow yourself to go within and feel centred.
- Tap the middle of the palm to activate the healing powers of the 11th chakra. Ask yourself what your mind, body and soul need right now.
- Tap each fingertip four or five times each. If you wish, start on your little finger, move to the ring finger and so on until you reach your thumb. Be creative and guided by what feels right for you.
- Do the same on your other hand, and tune in to how this makes you feel.
- Repeat on both hands again if you wish.
- Place your hands (palm chakras) on your body. Continue to breathe deeply and gently while your healing is activated. Sometimes your guides may tap your face or another body part to let you know they are around.
- Stay in this position for a few minutes.

Chapter 10

The psychic clairs

Clair means 'clear' in French. It's important to understand the seven psychic clairs as you will be tapping into them when you read palms. Everyone has the potential to psychically and intuitively use these extra senses to assist in accessing a greater wisdom.

Clairsentience (clear feeling)

Clairsentience, or clairempathy, is often the first and easiest clair sense to develop as it's linked to gut feelings and hunches. Most people are able to perceive what's going on around them, for instance if someone is sad or in physical pain or is not telling the truth. Your electrical nervous system has a psychic antenna that picks up different waves and vibrations of energy.

Clairvoyance (clear seeing)

Clairvoyant people may have prophetic visions or dreams of the future; this is known as precognition. You may experience psychic perceptions through vivid dreams, mental images or mini movies that flash in your awareness. You may also see colours around people, plants and animals, have a good sense of direction, easily visualise solutions to complications, be good at solving visual-spatial problems and like rearranging furniture.

Clairaudience (clear hearing)

People who play instruments, sing or write songs are usually strongly auditory, and therefore could be gifted in clairaudience. You may easily pick up the thoughts of people around you, which is known as mental telepathy. Once when I was in a school staffroom in a primary school where I taught I heard a sentence run through my mind; I was surprised, as I knew it wasn't my own thoughts. I realised it came from the lady sitting next to me as it directly related to a conversation we'd just had in another room. Luckily her thoughts were positive! If a spirit is speaking with you it may feel like it comes from outside your head and be in a slightly different octave to the vibration of your own thoughts. Depending on how developed your clairaudience is, you might be able to decipher whether the tone you are hearing is male or female. I sometimes hear specific words being said while at other times it's more like an energetic or telepathic communication I hear.

Clairtangency (clear touching)

Clairtangency is also known as psychometry, and involves the information you receive from touching an object, person or animal. It may come from a hug or handshake, from brushing up against someone or while sitting in a chair used by someone else. You may get psychic impressions when you are holding someone else's jewellery, article of clothing or a letter.

Claircognisance (clear knowing)

Claircognisance is wisdom or information in the form of ideas and concepts that suddenly come into your mind. Although it can be closely linked, this knowingness comes from somewhere other than your own thoughts and is of people or events you would not expect to have knowledge about. When you just seem to know something and it feels uncanny but is usually accurate, that is claircognisance.

Clairgustance (clear tasting)

Clairgustance and clairalience may be less commonly experienced than the other senses. Clairgustance is when you taste something even though there's nothing in your mouth; you are perceiving the energy of a substance from the spiritual realms. *Gustus* is a Latin word meaning 'to taste', 'to try' or 'to sample'.

Clairalience (clear smelling)

Clairalience or clairscent is smelling something even though the source of the smell is not evident and it is too subtle for other people to smell. It happened to me one day when a builder and I stood outside while he gave me his quote to repair my outdoor patio. I wasn't sure whether or not I would accept his quote but a strong scent of my favourite incense wafted over my nose. I was perplexed, as there was no incense being burned anywhere near where we were standing, but then I realised it was the universe's way of hinting at me to choose that particular builder. It was a fabulous sign from the universe, and of course I did go ahead and book him. He did a wonderful job for a brilliant price!

‿ The benefits of meditation ⁀

I like to meditate before I see clients, as it helps to activate my chakras and to centre and align my energy. I also love to do yoga or some type of exercise that physically moves my body. As the chakras are linked to the spine and nervous system movement helps them to cleanse, heal and expand. One day my client, Mary, arrived and settled into the chair in my office. 'I'm pregnant!' she said. 'Yes, I know, Mary,' I replied. She looked surprised. I handed her my notes from my morning meditation, in which she could clearly see the word 'pregnant' written. 'Oh, my God, how did you know?' she asked. I told her that in my meditation I had seen an image of her being pregnant.

Meditating allows your chakras to be more attuned to receiving energy and psychic information. Elsewhere in this book I provide simple ways to meditate and prepare yourself for palmistry readings.

Chapter 11
The chakras

It's vital to understand the chakras as the information will help you to become a more adept and tuned-in palm reader who can easily tap into the energy of the person you are reading for.

Crown chakra	Spirituality
Third eye chakra	Awareness
Throat chakra	Communication
Heart chakra	Love, healing
Solar plexus chakra	Wisdom, power
Sacral chakra	Sexuality, creativity
Root chakra	Basic trust

The chakras are delicate, sensitive energy areas that thrive and work well on the high vibration and potency of natural foods and drinks and positive thoughts. Each chakra has a different vibration, just like different chords on a guitar make a different sound. They are wheels that spin in a clockwise or anti-clockwise direction, allowing energy to flow in and out and storing information, but they can get blocked, especially if you do not move your body and process your emotions. For example, if you suppress anger the chakra wheel can become distorted and lose shape, then the stuck anger may affect your physical body. Your lungs hold the energy of grief, and if the grief is not released you may get chest pains or asthma because the chakra wheel will not turn as efficiently due to blocked emotions. Emotions are a natural part of life, but they are meant to move and channel through you so you can learn to love, heal, forgive and be more at peace in life.

Emotions = energy in motion

The 11th chakra, which is found in the hands and feet, is where you can absorb energy from around you. It's also a good place to release pent-up energy by putting your hands towards the earth and asking for any excess energy to be released. Placing the soles of your feet on the ground is an excellent way of cleansing your aura and energy field and recharging yourself. The chakras can receive and release energy depending on what is happening at the time in your body and soul.

Different websites and books will share different meanings of and explanations for the chakras. Personally, I refer to the 12 chakra system. See the table below for a summary of the 12 chakras.

Chakra		
1. Root/base: linked to the physical world such as home and work.	**Colour:** **Gland:** **Location:**	red adrenal hips, genitals
2. Sacral: linked to intimacy, dance and creative energy.	**Colour:** **Gland/s:** **Location:**	orange ovaries, testes abdomen
3. Solar plexus: linked to childhood, the inner child and fun.	**Colour:** **Gland:** **Location:**	yellow pancreas solar plexus
4. Heart: linked to compassion, fears and joy.	**Colours:** **Gland:** **Location:**	green, pink, gold heart heart
5. Throat: linked to communication and expression.	**Colour:** **Gland:** **Location:**	blue thyroid throat

Chakra		
6. Third eye: linked to psychic sight and visions.	**Colours:** **Gland:** **Location:**	purple, indigo pituitary forehead
7. Crown: linked to your ability to tap into a higher realm, to healing and connection to oneness.	**Colours:** **Gland:** **Location:**	white, clear, violet pineal crown
8. Records (past lives, Akashic): linked to other lifetimes and your soul plan.	**Colours:** **Gland:** **Location:**	silver, ultraviolet, black thymus 4 cm above the head
9. Soul: linked to your wiser self, passion and purpose.	**Colours:** **Muscle:** **Location:**	gold, infrared diaphragm arm's length above the head
10. Grounding: linked to being solid and focused on this earth plane.	**Colours:** **Affects:** **Location:**	brown, yellow, green bones 30–100 cm below the feet

Chakra		
11. Transmutation: linked to the ability to manifest, transform and be empowered.	**Colour:** **Gland:** **Location:**	pink connective tissue, meridians palms and soles of the feet
12. Purpose: linked to your higher being and guides, who nudge you on your path to help you find freedom and purpose.	**Colour:** **Gland:** **Location:**	no colour as these are points on body 32 points various points around the body

(Source: Cindi Dale, *The Complete Book of Chakra Healing*, Llewellyn Worldwide, Minnesota, 2010)

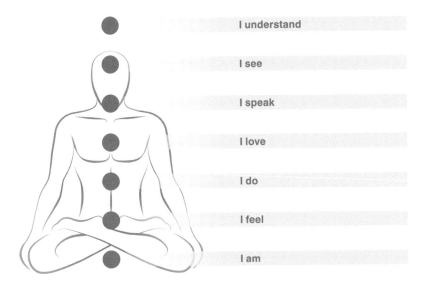

I understand

I see

I speak

I love

I do

I feel

I am

These exercises will help you to train your third eye to be more active. Along with your two physical eyes you have a third eye in between your eyebrows that 'sees' on another level. I have done the exercises below with many clients and students and have obtained amazing results. I also do them before I see clients to help activate my third eye and retrieve information more easily from the higher realms. Enjoy practising!

Exercise 8: *opening your third eye and higher chakras*

- Relax and breathe deeply 10 times into your diaphragm and abdomen. Feel grounded to the earth below you by imagining your energy going into the earth and then back up to the sky. Close your eyes and repeat several times.
- As you breathe in and out imagine that a golden light of energy is filling up the inside of your body and the space you are in. Understand this golden light is calming, soothing and protecting you with divine love and essence, and that all

of your chakras are filled with love and high vibration.

- Ask your third eye to open for you, and ask the seventh, eighth and ninth chakras to be open and activated. You may feel energy in between your eyebrows as tingles, warmth and pressure as your body responds to your request. Be aware of any other sensations in your body.
- Take your attention back to the area in between your eyebrows. You may sense that it feels different as the golden light of energy will have helped your third eye and higher chakras to expand, heal and open.

Visualisation practice

- Imagine you are opening the door to your home. Walk in and notice what you see: look around at the furniture and notice the colours in the room. Next, imagine you are in a movie theatre watching a big red screen but you notice that it changes to a silvery blue colour. You see different images and colours on the screen. Be aware of colours, shapes, smells, sounds, movement and activity and take note of what forms on the inner third eye screen in your mind.

- Ask to be shown something on the screen that happened yesterday and see what it looks like. Ask for the images to be clearer and more focused if you require more clarity. Ask what will happen tomorrow and see what comes up on your screen. Keep practising to strengthen your third eye and other chakras.

Advanced exercise

Practise using your third eye and higher chakras by looking at trees and sensing tree spirits and elemental beings around them. The more you do these exercises the more you will have visions and insights. Also look at the auras of people, animals and flowers: you'll be surprised by the colours and shapes around all living things.

Chapter 12

Tips for performing a palmistry reading

These tips will help you to navigate a reading. The most important to remember is to refrain from saying negative or unproductive things to a client as words can stay for years in a person's head and affect their mental health and well-being. Tread very carefully when passing information on to a client: they will view you as an adviser and confidant, and you should take that role seriously. People are great manifestors, so aim to empower your clients so they can turn challenging things in their life around. Refer your clients to counselling or phone help lines if they require more assistance and support.

Be a fabulous guide for your clients. Be present with your heart, your wisdom and compassion. Go forth and strive!

Lines talk

I love the way different people read palms. One palm reader wisely said to me, 'Allow the lines to talk to you.' I agree with this sentiment, as tuning in to the lines on the palm will allow the person's energy to share its meaning and message with you. There will always be so much positive information the hand has to give you.

We are all creators of our own lives, and we can create magic in our lives by being more conscious, aware and heart-based. Our aim as palm readers is not to imprint fear or negative messages into our clients, as every message should be given with love and kindness. This will help the client know they can profoundly change their lives through their positive actions, thoughts and deeds.

I sometimes share information with a client in a claircognisant (clear knowing) way. I once started telling a client about tantra and heart connections with her husband and was wondering why I had mentioned it to her, but she was delighted as she said she and her husband were having intimacy problems and she needed to know where to go for help in this area of her relationship. Sometimes the guides will enable information to channel through you that is necessary for your client to hear.

Our palms reveal what ingredients we need in order to create success and heal the burdens of our past. There is so much love and wisdom in the universe, and tapping into that from your heart and soul helps to put your controlling, fear-based, manipulative ego in check so you are in charge of your ego and it is not in charge of you!

Boundaries

Boundaries are important for yourself and others. Only share information if you have permission from the person for whom you are doing the reading. Not everyone is interested in the psychic information you may receive, so be careful if you are at a dinner party! Respect the feelings of others and only share any pearls of wisdom or insight with them after asking if it's okay to do so. Remember to share insights with love and good intentions.

During the reading

I suggest you become familiar with the exercises in this book to help you build your psychic muscle and become more in touch with your heart when giving a reading.

It's a real privilege when someone comes to you for a reading. You need to remember that some people put

on a brave face but underneath they may be sensitive and feeling delicate, and an inappropriate phrase or inaccurate information can really damage someone who is imbalanced or who suffers from anxiety or depression. Be mindful of the power of your words and share any words you have with sincerity.

Some palmists I know prefer not to read for family or close friends as they feel their close relationship can affect the reading. Do what feels right for you.

'People are extremely vulnerable when they offer you their palm to read. Never rush to make an observation, take your time, be gentle, be kind, but be honest. — John Fincham

The following is a list of things you may use when undertaking a palmistry reading; you may use some of them, all of them or none of them:

- magnifying glass
- candle
- flower incense spray
- aromatherapy oils
- relaxing music

- oracle and inspirational cards
- a cushion for the person's hand to rest on (or use a table)
- palmistry checklist (see Appendix I)
- lamp or torch
- pen and paper
- comfortable chairs
- business cards

Some clients ask for a pen and paper to record information, and some ask if they can record the session on their phone or a mini recorder. Some palmists will not allow their sessions to be recorded, but I am happy for clients to do that if they wish to. I know of some palmists who record their own sessions and send the recording to clients afterwards. One psychic medium told me she no longer allows clients to record the sessions as she once told a lady her husband was no good for her and that she should leave him, then the next week a huge man turned up for a reading saying he was the husband! This angry man had heard the recording and wanted to know why the medium had told his wife to leave him. The medium told me the session with him ended well but it made her realise that she did not want to be put in that position again.

When I do a palmistry reading my clients put their palms on a cushion; at psychic fairs I use a small table. I like to sit diagonally from the client at a corner of the table so that we are closer to each other and the person does not have to stretch their arms too far across the table.

Remember to do the four-step activation sequence (see page 36) prior to seeing your client. Sometimes at expos it can be noisy, so I may hold the person's hands to connect and centre us both. I ask the person to close their eyes and breathe slowly as I say aloud words such as:

'As we breathe deeply and relax we allow the energy
of peace, love and tranquillity to fill us.
We open our hearts up to the magnificence of life.
May this session be full of wisdom, divinity and
pure connection to spirit. Thank you.'

A prayer such as this helps me to centre and align with the client's energies, and I hope it enables them to do the same.

Sometimes I get my client to hold a crystal, especially if they are sad or low in energy. I also often hold crystals to replenish my energy field. I like to use clear quartz or rose quartz, but there are many different crystals that you may be drawn to using. Imagining a huge crystal around your energy field can be just as powerful.

Remember that your spirit guides are waiting to help you. Call them in to assist you and share their energy, love and wisdom with you. Ask for your chakras and clairs to open up and help you. Sometimes you may hear, feel, know and see things. Also ask that you see a movie type of image, as if you are watching a TV screen, if you need more clarity and information.

Once while undertaking a reading for a client named Mary a movie scene appeared in my mind of a young girl cutting her wrists. I delicately shared with Mary what I had seen. She confirmed that her daughter harmed herself through cutting her skin but that she was receiving counselling and getting help. The guides came through with comforting messages for Mary.

Use the scrying exercise (see page 122) to tap in to the energy of the palms. Many clients ask, 'Which hand do you want to look at?' I find out which is their writing (dominant) hand then let them know this hand represents the future and later half of life. I explain how the non-dominant hand represents genetics and what they bring into this lifetime, and inform them that looking at both hands is important in the overall palmistry reading.

At the end of the reading I like the person to randomly choose an inspirational card to take home. These cards, which you can purchase from bookstores or online, usually have beautiful sayings on them.

⤚ The heart line ⤙

This story outlines how our palm lines can reveal changes that happen in our lifetime.

Sunya was a 35-year-old woman from Malaysia. The heart line on her non-dominant hand was broken but the heart line on her right dominant hand was perfectly formed and had a beautiful curve in it. I tuned in to the energy of the heart lines and said that part of her destiny was to heal her broken heart and her beliefs about love, forgiveness and betrayal.

Sunya told me that when she was younger she had been through a horrible divorce and had later married an Australian man she had met at work. She was very happy in this current marriage, and said that her husband helped her to believe in love and kindness as he was such a good man.

I find it interesting that the unhealed trauma and grief from the generations of family before us can be carried down energetically, which can happen if there are unresolved issues from our ancestors that have not been fully healed. Sunya's left non-dominant hand was also connected to the burdens of her family ancestors.

I could see that Sunya would overcome her broken heart, as her dominant hand revealed a strong heart line. Sunya also had a happy sun line, which supported the findings that life in her future was bound to be happier and more abundant for her.

Sunya told me she adored her husband but was struggling to find a way to balance her home and work life. She was financially supporting her family overseas, which put extra pressure on her. We discussed what she could do to create a more centred and happy life for herself and her family. Sunya left the session more in touch with what she needed to do over the next few months.

Cleansing and grounding techniques

These cleansing and grounding techniques will help your energy body remain strong, resilient and clear:

- Imagine a waterfall cascading from overhead and gently cleansing your entire being.
- Spray flower essences around or use drops.
- Hold a crystal and meditate.

- Ask and pray/affirm that you release the person for whom you are reading with love and you wish them the best on their journey.
- Put your feet on the earth and allow the earth's energy to ground and rebalance your energy field.
- Point your palms (11th chakra) down towards the ground, asking that excess energy be released and that you breathe clear, healing energy into your soul.
- Have a sea salt or Epsom salt bath (½ cup of either in the water) to relax and cleanse your mind, body and soul. Staying in the bath for at least 20 minutes will help you to gain the benefits of the bath and will allow your brain waves and nervous system to go into a deeply relaxed state. You could add a few drops of lavender or some other aromatherapy oils to the bath. Some people put in a chamomile teabag to help them relax.
- Play music that you find soothing and calming.
- Lie down and imagine you are cocooned in a beautiful crystal dome that will transform dense energy and turn it into light, peaceful energy.
- Laugh, dance, smile, hug, play!

Chapter 13
Sample readings

I have been heard many times saying in my palmistry courses: 'Allow the palm to speak to you.'

When students anxiously tell me they can't get anything I guide them to slow down, breathe and hear the quiet whispers within: it's here the answers of the cosmos reside. The student is usually amazed at the depth of information, wisdom and answers they receive, and are enthralled by the magic of reading palms!

Reading 1: dominant right hand

Begin with the four-step activation sequence (see page 36) to open up your intuitive abilities, then:

- Open your third eye and upper chakras. Tap into your heart chakra and guides.
- Take a look at the hand image.
- Scry the palm and see what you receive about this person. Blend with the energy and personality of the hand.

Sample 1 Palm

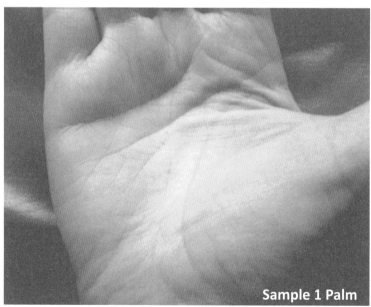

Sample 1 Palm

- Is this person male or female?
- What are their interests and hobbies?
- What do the major lines reveal to you?
- What do the minor lines reveal to you?
- Look at the palmistry checklist on page 167 to help guide you.
- Record your information and insights. (See Appendix II for my reading of this palm.)

Reading 2: dominant right hand

Begin with the four-step activation sequence (see page 36) to open up your intuitive abilities. Then:

- Open your third eye and upper chakras. Tap into your heart chakra and guides.
- Take a look at the hand image.
- Scry the palm and see what you receive about this person. Blend with the energy and personality of the hand.
- Is this person male or female?
- What are their interests and hobbies?
- What do the major lines reveal to you?
- What do the minor lines reveal to you?

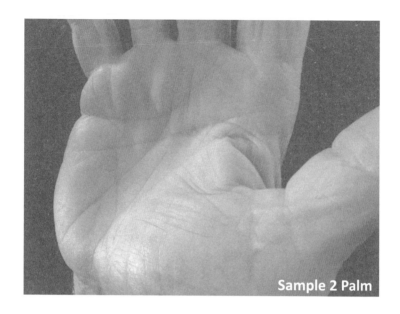

Sample 2 Palm

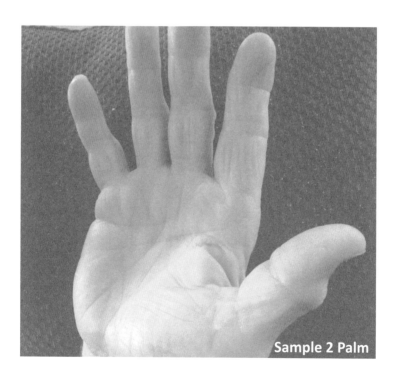

Sample 2 Palm

- Look at the palmistry checklist on page 167 to help guide you.
- Record your information and insights. (See Appendix III for my reading of this palm.)

Final note

Remember to be gentle with yourself and others, and that the more you read palms the more you will excel in this beautiful and unique skill. We are all born with gifts and talents; continue to cultivate your gifts and talents with ongoing dedication, commitment and focus.

I wish you all the best. Peace to you. — Anna

APPENDIX I
Palmistry checklist

This checklist is a useful guide that you can refer to when doing readings to help you remember which areas to focus on.

Name:

Date of birth:

Today's date:

Left ● Right ● handed	Comments
Shape of the hand • Fire, air, earth, water	
Fingers • Length, sections, spacing, tips, nails, colour of the hand	
Thumb • Will, logic • Low set (90 degrees) or high set • Supple or stiff	

Lines
- Health line (Mercury/hepatica line)
- Fate line (Saturn/destiny/career line)
- Intuition line (line of Uranus)
- Apollo line (sun line)
- Union lines (relationship line)
- Children lines
- Travel lines
- Rascette/bracelet lines
- Mars line (sister line)
- Via lascivia line (poison/allergy line/line of Neptune)
- Line of sympathy
- Ring/seal of Solomon
- Loyalty line

Markings
- Triangles, squares, crosses, grilles/nets, islands, dots, circles, tridents/forks, tassels, chains, breaks, stars, influence lines, branches (upward/downward lines)

Other features

- St Andrew's Cross
- Angel path
- Girdle of Venus
- Sydney line
- Family chain
- Mystic cross
- Simian line
- Medical stigmata
- Psychic cross

Mounts

- Jupiter
- Saturn
- Apollo
- Mercury
- Luna
- Venus
- Neptune
- Mars 1
- Mars 2
- Mars plain

APPENDIX II
Outline of reading 1

The images are of a dominant right hand of a 51-year-old female, Joan, who is a teacher, therapist and healer and lives in Canberra, Australia. She has one daughter. Joan has a psychic cross in the middle of her angel path area, highlighting her psychic and intuitive abilities. She also has a ring of Solomon on her Jupiter mount, indicating her natural inclination to help others.

Joan's head line is separate from her life line, which indicates an impulsive, independent and strong-minded individual. There are teacher squares on the Jupiter mount and a curved heart line, indicating compassion and connection.

Joan has a slightly longer Jupiter (index) finger, which represents leadership ability. Her fate line starts near the wrist and there is another fate line coming from the Luna mount and going up towards the Saturn (middle) finger. This represents the different career path Joan took in her 40s in the area of healing and spiritual arts. Joan has a writer's fork at the end of her head line, which shows her natural interest in writing. Joan has published a book and loves yoga, reading and the beach.

Joan has a low-set thumb, indicating determination and focus. She has two lines on the sun mount, representing two main areas of success in life. Joan has a medical stigmata, which highlights her healing work in reiki and as a therapist.

APPENDIX III
Outline of reading 2

The images are of a dominant right hand belonging to a 75-year-old male who lives in Wagga Wagga, New South Wales, Australia. (It is actually my dad, Noel Comerford!) He has an unusual line on his palm – a Sydney line – that is where the head line extends all the way across the palm. This line is not classed as a simian line as he still has a separate heart line.

Noel is a very determined and focused person who owned spare car parts businesses. He enjoys lawn bowls, has a sweet tooth, is a family man and was born in Dublin, Ireland. An only child, he moved to Australia with his mum when he was a teenager. He married my mum Maria and had six children, and has grandchildren and one great grandchild.

Noel's head line is separate from his life line, which is only seen in 20 per cent of hands. A separated head line indicates an impulsive, independent and strong-minded individual. There is a psychic cross in the middle of the angel path area and some teacher squares on the Jupiter mount; Noel used to teach night classes at a local technical school. There is a curved heart line, indicating compassion and connection.

Noel has a longer Apollo (ring) finger, which represents initiative and drive. The fate line starts at the Luna mount and flows towards Saturn, indicating overseas travel. There is a writer's fork at the end of the head line, showing a natural interest in writing and expression; Noel loves to record his daily events in his writing journal. He has an earth-shaped hand, which as he is now retired suits him as he loves to build and tinker on his farm. The Mercury (little) finger is slightly apart from the Apollo digit, signifying his independence and enjoyment of his own freedom and space.

Acknowledgements

Thanks to the all-powerful divine cosmos for guiding me to write, play and be!

I self-published this book in 2016, then Rockpool Publishing offered me a publishing contract. My book got a facelift and was lovingly updated and revamped, and I am grateful to the dynamic duo Lisa Hanrahan and Paul Dennett and their amazing team for supporting my passion for spirituality and palmistry.

Huge thanks go to my supportive parents, Noel and Maria, who I was blessed to have in this lifetime. They are always encouraging me and cheering me on. Thanks to my gorgeous brothers and sister and their families for being kind and caring. To my daughter Kira, whose wonderful smile and kind heart make me believe anything is possible.

To Reecey, who has shown me that strength is within each of us. To my beloved Billy, who listens with joy, warmth and enthusiasm: I am so grateful for your loving presence. To his sons Jordan and Isaac, who have shown me that magic does happen.

Thank *you* for reading this book, for seeking the wisdom in your heart. I honour you. Stay strong: we need your light and compassion.

About the author

Anna Comerford is an international psychic medium, naturopath, herbalist, crystal healer, yoga and meditation teacher, reiki master, hypnotherapist, coach, tarot lover, astrologer and palmist with Bachelor degrees in Education and Health Science. She has taught in primary schools for the past 35 years, has spoken at seminars both in Australia and overseas, runs the School of Higher Learning and along with this book wrote *The Spiritual Guidebook*.

Australian psychic of the year in 2017, Anna has appeared on psychic TV in Australia and has seen thousands of clients across the world. Anna is passionate

about linking science and spirituality in ways that are easy to understand and knows that by understanding the magic of spirit and how it works in our lives we can better know ourselves and others.

Her mission is to teach the power of love, connection and intuition and she is keen to spread the message that *everybody* is psychic and has amazing intuitive abilities. Anna firmly believes that individuals can make profound changes in their lives that can greatly impact the world in which we live.

annacomerford.com